REVISED AND UPDATED

# THE TRUTH ABOUT
# TEACHING

## What I *Wish* the Veterans Had Told Me

# COLEEN ARMSTRONG

## Published in Partnership with Inspiring Teachers

JOSSEY-BASS
A Wiley Imprint
www.josseybass.com

Published by Jossey-Bass
A Wiley Imprint
989 Market Street, San Francisco, CA 94103-1741—www.josseybass.com

Jossey-Bass books and products are available through most bookstores. To contact Jossey-Bass directly call our Customer Care Department within the U.S. at 800-956-7739, outside the U.S. at 317-572-3986, or fax 317-572-4002.

Jossey-Bass also publishes its books in a variety of electronic formats. Some content that appears in print may not be available in electronic books.

**Library of Congress Cataloging-in-Publication Data**

Armstrong, Coleen, 1946-
    The truth about teaching : what I wish the veterans had told me / Coleen Armstrong. – Rev. and updated.
        p. cm.
    "Published in Partnership with Inspiring Teachers."
    Includes bibliographical references and index.
    ISBN 978-0-470-50072-9 (hardback)
    1. Teaching–United States. 2. First year teachers–In-service training–United States.
I. Title.
    LB1775.2.A748 2009
    371.102–dc22

                        2009028275

Printed in the United States of America
FIRST EDITION

*HB Printing*        10 9 8 7 6 5 4 3 2 1

# Contents

Inspiring Teachers is a teacher-created organization dedicated to empowering and inspiring educators. Our vision is to help teachers create quality learner-centered classrooms and improve student success. To meet this vision, we offer a variety of print and free online resources including our website, www.inspiringteachers.com, a free weekly teaching tips newsletter, Ask A Mentor service, practical guides for teachers, and staff development workshops. Each element of our support system can be used individually or in conjunction with other parts. We are here to let educators know they are not alone. We've been there! We understand the daily life of a classroom teacher—stressful, overwhelming, and often lonely. We are here to help ease the stress, offer a listening ear, and lend a helpful hand to any teacher in need. You can contact us at info@inspiringteachers.com.

*To Emma, Ethan, Bennett, and Abigail*

*May you always encounter kind, loving, and inspiring teachers.*

# THE TRUTH ABOUT
# TEACHING

# 1

# Getting Started

"*I'm always stirred by the tremendous decency and kindness of teachers. They are good, solid human beings who do their jobs day after day with love and affection. Their work is not proficiency and outcome, it's poetry and ministry.*"

**—Jonathan Kozol**

This book is a love letter to new teachers. By new, I mean anyone with fewer than five years' experience. And by a love letter, I mean an acknowledgment that you probably haven't received anywhere near the credit you deserve for finding the courage to become a teacher. I'll bet plenty of loved ones tried to talk you out of it. Yet you forged ahead. That took pluck, daring, valor . . . even a kind of heroism.

So I want to begin by providing some reassurance that whatever difficulties you may encounter probably aren't due to what you'd otherwise think were your own personal shortcomings. Take my word for it: rough moments happen to all of us. Yet we survive—and thrive. So will you.

Much has changed since I began my career in 1968. Back then, first-year teachers were thrown to the wolves with little or no guidance and then left to thrash about desperately on their own with no intervention. Today, because you receive far more rigorous and intensive preparation than we did, along with plenty of classroom monitoring early on, you might assume that the day-to-day realities of the profession would feel far less like being doused with repeated buckets of cold water.

But I doubt it.

No beginning teacher can be anything less than shocked at finding his lunch break so short that it's impossible to check his mailbox, go to the restroom, *and* scarf down a hot dog. (He must choose one, perhaps two out of three.) Or that if his school is not air-conditioned (many still aren't), heat waves and indoor temperatures reaching ninety-five to a hundred degrees can linger through late October. Or that every weekend will likely be spent grading, bookkeeping, and lesson planning.

During your first few months in the classroom, the disillusionment factor can be huge. There are so many students to meet and get to know, so many lessons to prepare in excruciating detail (some principals require that plans be turned in a week in advance), so many baffling dictates to follow ("During a fire drill, exit through the east door." *Which way is east?*).

But I believe that disillusionment leads to dropping out only when you feel as if the problems are yours alone. This book is a testament to the fact that you are most definitely not alone. After reading it, you'll never again say, "I thought it was just me."

My intention here is to alert you to the thorny issues that no one else wants to talk about. I often call them educational blasphemy, because bringing them up usually results in killing the messenger, or at least a venomous verbal attack designed to shut him up forever.

Some may accuse me of sounding cynical. But I want to shed a bright light and save you years of grinding your teeth in frustration by learning everything the hard way. So here you'll find an acknowledgment of a problem—followed by a reassurance, an anecdote, or in most cases, a remedy.

I hope this book will help you feel less isolated and more turbocharged, more convinced than ever that teaching is your true calling. And I hope that someday, long before you've completed your thirty-year stellar career with your mental and physical health still intact, you too will have lots of funny, tragic, heartwarming tales to tell.

Meanwhile, here's my first advice nugget. It may well be the most essential one of all.

# Never lose sight of your own power.

Teaching in our K–12 schools is the world's noblest, most important, most invigorating, and most satisfying job. But you'll have moments when you'll feel whipped, drained, stranded, defenseless, used up, and spit out. And utterly, completely powerless.

That last word, *powerless,* is the one I want to contradict. Nothing could be further from the truth.

The most essential component of effective education isn't a sparkling new classroom. It isn't spacious whiteboards, computer technology, or updated textbooks. It isn't plenty of glistening, sturdy desks or freshly painted walls. Although such accoutrements are certainly wonderful, there's only one variable that's absolutely essential to the learning process: you. The teacher.

You are where every lesson begins and ends. You run the show. You set the tone. You create the camaraderie. You dictate whether your kids look forward to your class—or loathe it. You can be either a soothing, reassuring influence—or a sniping, critical one. You can, in fact, save a child's life; if not physically, then surely emotionally and intellectually. Or you can let her fall through the cracks.

> I touch the future. I teach.
> **—CHRISTA MCAULIFFE**

The choice is yours. And although for most of us it's an easy one to make, its daily implementation will continually be a challenge. Despite your best intentions, you'll be crippled by a shortage of time and energy, frazzled by constant interruptions, frustrated by students who huff that they'd rather be anywhere else but in school, and infuriated by taxpayers who think that teachers only work part-time.

Yet somehow, thousands upon thousands of us rise above such handicaps and misconceptions. No wonder observers are awestruck when they realize they're watching (or once, long ago, had the privilege of watching) a truly talented classroom presence. On some level, they must realize how much self-assurance, dedication, charisma, and hard work that requires.

As for us, we understand what a privilege it is.

No wonder so many professionals in other fields confess that they always secretly yearned to be teachers. There is no more powerful place to be than in a classroom, where mutual esteem and genuine affection between a teacher and his or her students are palpable.

It's often said that a child is lucky if she encounters one dynamic, inspiring teacher during her entire twelve years of school. That's the bad news. The good news is . . . one is all it takes to change everything.

Wouldn't it be awesome if that one turned out to be *you*?

# 2

# The Profession and the Politics

*"There is no real teacher who in practice does not believe in the existence of the soul, or in a magic that acts on it through speech."*

**—Allan Bloom**

# Remember that you're on a divine mission.

In your heart you already know this. You wouldn't be a teacher if you didn't understand on some level that you've been handpicked by the universe to carry out the most sacred trust on Earth—preparing the next generation to take its rightful place in the world and giving them the skills they'll need to run it successfully. Intimidated by the impact of it all? You should be. If you weren't, you'd be arrogant—and arrogance is one of the worst traits for anyone to carry into a classroom. It hinders growth, change, learning . . . and, most essentially, empathy.

Occasionally someone will regard teaching fourth grade as a mere stepping-stone toward something better (read: higher paying). Although these folks (I met only two throughout my entire career) may well have something significant to offer in terms of administration, they still need to start, so to speak, in the trenches. Most who "advance" eventually regard those early years spent interacting with the kiddoes as some of their most cherished—which is as it should be.

If by chance none of this applies to you, if you've selected the teaching profession for the security, as something to fall back on until you discover your true talent, or for the "long" breaks, then please do everyone, including yourself, a favor, and go elsewhere. We desperately need more fine teachers—but there's no room for anyone who's less than totally committed. This is a tough, demanding assignment, with enormous challenges and even greater rewards. It's not a place to hide out, relax, or bide your time.

# You also have a hidden agenda.

You were hired to teach sixth-grade math or tenth-grade biology. But it won't take long before you realize that your real reason for being there is something much more fundamental and long lasting—to coach, to bolster, and to reassure. To escort your students with love and compassion into adulthood. To provide a safe, secure sounding board. To be a stable influence. To model honesty and integrity.

In a few cases, you may be the only reliable, rational, solid, and steady adult in your kids' lives. And if you think that's an exaggeration, let's meet again in five years, after you've gotten to know a few hundred of them, and we'll talk.

I can tell you this much with certainty: teachers are probably the only people they'll ever meet, besides a small handful of close friends and family members, who are happy to extend themselves beyond measure for someone else's benefit, rather than their own—and who ask absolutely nothing in return.

"In the world of books I am a late bloomer. My first book was published when I was 66, my second when I was 69. So what took (me) so long? I was teaching, that's what took me so long. In four different New York City public high schools.
**—FRANK MCCOURT**

# Get ready to work harder than you ever have in your entire life.

This is not a job for one person—but you'll have to pretend that it is. That's the only way you'll be able to deal with being your own administrative assistant, researcher, scribe, custodian, and gofer. You'll be keeping records that will rival the IRS, along with files upon files of teaching materials. You'll be planning lessons, grading papers, and composing tests far into the night and probably every weekend. You'll be carrying around inside your head the personality profiles of as many as 170 unique, individual, precious human beings. You'll even be wiping down boards and inventorying and storing your own textbooks. All while the rest of the world tells you how easy your job is. Which brings me to . . .

# The three-month vacation is largely a myth.

You may well spend those ten weeks teaching summer school or supervising band practice, taking classes for recertification and to upgrade your skills (often at your own expense), writing your master's thesis, attending seminars, pruning your lesson plans, polishing your tests and worksheets, brushing up on your subject matter, getting your classroom ready for fall—or quite possibly all of the above. You may also be tutoring for extra cash or taking on odd jobs to pay the bills.

You must try, however, to reserve at least a couple of weeks to rest and regenerate. Brush aside all uninformed remarks like, "Must be nice to have all that time off." People who say such things not only don't understand the profession's demands but also will never have the immeasurable impact on future generations that you will.

# You'll pay for most of your own supplies.

That includes resource materials, videos and DVDs, CDs, bulletin board posters and signs, storage bins and file cabinets, red marking pens, a decent chair (unless you want to develop serious back problems), a podium (if you like that sort of thing; I didn't), paper and pencils for kids who refuse or "forget" to bring anything with them to class . . . Many of us cave in on that particular issue and keep stashes in our desk drawers just to stop the constant headaches.

And this is embarrassing to admit, but because I had so much trouble getting my reluctant learners to pay for supplemental paperbacks, in my later years I finally just bought entire classroom sets myself. Oh, well. At least it was tax deductible. Save every receipt.

# You'll learn far more than you'll ever teach.

Teachers are fond of saying that you never really know something until you teach it, but the issue runs far deeper than that. This is one of those upside-down life lessons that will dawn on you very early in your career. There is no faster way to learn about human nature and what motivates people than to work with kids. Their emotions are so out there and easily readable that you'll grow to spot a good defense mechanism, rationalization, projection, or passive-aggressive move a mile away. (And that's just in the field of psychology. Don't even get me started on socialization, bonding, or mating rituals.) Successful learning has a lot to do with being receptive to it—and oddly, you'll become your own most receptive audience, eagerly learning new things every day about both your subject matter and your students.

> A little learning, indeed may be a dangerous thing, but the want of learning is a calamity to any people.
> **—FREDERICK DOUGLASS**

# If you go in thinking that it's not your job to be mother, father, or psychoanalyst, you'll be proven wrong again and again.

When a kid has a problem, chances are the first person she will turn to is her teacher. The reasons? You're accessible. You're wise. You're warm. You care. Kids can spot those four characteristics a mile away. Be flattered—and grateful. It means you're doing something right.

Besides, most of your role will be to listen and nod.

At the same time, know when to call in the big guns. Any time a kid begins to speak of suicide, drug or sexual abuse, violent impulses, self-mutilation, or hearing voices in his head, don't try to handle it yourself. The issue is far bigger than you. See an administrator immediately. He or she will have a list of resources and people to contact.

# You'll be expected to adjust to everyone. No one will adjust to you.

A fellow teacher told me once that on that first day filled with meetings, she was always astonished to see everyone on the support staff stand up and declare to the assembled group, "Here's what you all need to do to get along with me." Which meant, in essence, to make *their* jobs easier. Everyone. Administrators, guidance counselors, custodians, paraprofessionals, food service workers, administrative assistants substitutes, bus drivers . . . (Okay, maybe not bus drivers.)

A parole officer knocked on my door one day and demanded to see one of my students. Immediately. "He's working on his English assignment," I protested. "Well," he snorted, "this is the only chance I have to check on him." The saddest part of this was that he'd intruded on me *with* the office's approval.

I'm not sure when valuable classroom time became such easy pickings for everyone else on the planet, from hall monitors to military recruiters, but unfortunately that's where we are now—at about the same time that expectations have become nearly unachievable. In desperation, I finally began locking my door and ignoring the persistent tap-tap-tapping. Other than that, I don't have a solution, only a suggestion that it's time for a serious wake-up call. If we're assigned an essential task, then others need to stop violating the learning process every twenty-five seconds.

# This job will both harden and soften you.

Get ready to be simultaneously enraged at the vast scope of your job and at the way public policy continually devalues your efforts despite mountains of lip service—and moved to tears by the vulnerability and intense needs of so many kids with whom you work. What you will begin to suspect is true: few people care about them as much as you do, because you get to know them personally as the talented, yearning, multifaceted individuals they are.

Politicians and taxpayers tend to see children only as abstracts, which is why schools must continually scrape by financially, generation after generation. (I believe that everyone running for public office should first spend six weeks as a seventh-grade reading teacher. That would quickly turn all of those abstracts into concretes.)

Imagine a doctor needing to purchase his own surgical tools and also being accused of incompetence every time the patient didn't get better. Wouldn't she be irritated?

You're gifted with a painful vision: the ability to see what could take place educationally if we had enough time, space, manpower, and facilities. The frustration of seeing where we are versus where we could be will endure throughout your career.

What's more, just about the time you consider chucking it all, some kid taps you on the shoulder and asks, "Can I talk to you? I don't know where else to turn."

And your heart melts.

# Schools have hierarchies.

Academic, college-bound, and honors-level students are generally perceived as more serious about their educations and therefore more desirable to teach than average or below-average kids. But the first time you're assigned a class where your students are struggling, you'll discover that it's all a matter of perspective. Not only do these kids come up with some amazing insights, you'll also run into your share of talented writers, history buffs, computer wizards, and political pundits.

Not everyone can be an honor roll star. In many American families, just earning a high school diploma—never mind college—is still an enormous accomplishment.

So how should we define a triumph? I once saw a senior boy break down in tears two weeks before graduation because his grades were marginal and his status was still in question. "My parents expect me to do better than just a GED," he wept. "It's so much pressure!" And for him, it was.

Perhaps success, then, is best measured in terms of starting points. A child who has been told all his life that finishing high school is a lofty, nearly unachievable goal will probably believe it. Part of your job will be to convince her that she can aspire to a much higher level than she's been groomed to believe. It does no good to cloud that endeavor with prejudgments.

And speaking of hierarchies, I don't need to tell you that introducing yourself in a public setting as a teacher of advanced-placement calculus will widen more eyes than telling people you teach basic math. Yet we all know that some of the most inspiring educators wind up in some very humble places and positions.

> Few citizens really know what's going on in their schools. They settle for the familiar and ignore the substance.
> **—TED SIZER**

# You'll get three-year-olds and thirty-year-olds in the same class—and both will be remarkably easy to spot.

The three-year-olds will protest, complain, and waste truckloads of energy trying to circumvent you and get out of doing any work. In short, they'll exhaust you. The thirty-year-olds will quietly do as they're instructed, often completing assignments faster than you ever thought possible and then wait patiently until the "children" finish up. Only rarely will they even comment on the disparity to their peers. Occasionally they'll talk to you, though. Those conversations will invigorate you. Eventually some satisfying friendships develop.

Oddly, this division has little to do with basic intelligence or background. I've seen some very bright, advantaged kids turn out to be incredible whiners—and some who have every right to be defensive and angry rise to higher-than-normal expectations.

# Smart kids still get placed on slow or average tracks.

There's nothing more frustrating than seeing a sharp, talented kid sitting contentedly in a basic-level class. You have a bored student on your hands, someone who may decide to devote a huge amount of energy to trying to make your life difficult. In elementary classes you'll spot this discrepancy early, through astonishingly well-written themes or test scores indicating giftedness.

Talk to their parents. These children need and deserve added enrichment. They must find a passion, or they can grow bored, restless, and turned off about the entire educational process. It's an ideal opportunity for you to become a friend and advocate.

> "I think education is power. I think that being able to communicate with people is power. One of my main goals on this planet is to encourage people to empower themselves."
> **—OPRAH WINFREY**

# Schools will never run like businesses—nor should they.

Businesses limit how many people they can cram into a single room; classrooms don't. Businesses are allowed to decide whom they'll hire and when to fire unproductive workers; teachers aren't. Businesses can demand that workers toe the line according to their specifications; schools can't.

Every time a student spent an entire semester doing no work whatsoever (or worse, being continually absent), and my pleading calls to his parents went ignored—and then a week before graduation they called, insisting that I "find a way" to pass him (based on what?)—I fervently wished that schools did run more like businesses. But then I reconsidered. We continually embrace all comers, regardless of their backgrounds, resources, or attitudes. Children are not capital. I wasn't running an assembly line. Bottom-line profit was not king. Thank goodness.

# Vouchers were never the answer.

First of all, private and charter schools don't have to deal with unfunded mandates that gobble down huge revenues. Second, they can be selective about whom they admit—and they can kick out the hard-core troublemakers whenever they wish. Third, they tend to have very involved parents, something public schools can only dream about.

Do we want our own kids to have the best possible education? Absolutely. Do we want every kid to have the same advantages? Well, if we look at the widely disparate school conditions across our country, we can only conclude that we apparently do not. That is what must change. Hey, guys, charter schools for everyone! Cream-of-the-crop teaching methods for everyone! Concerned, dedicated parents for everyone! Is that really too much to ask? So far . . . yes.

# Educational "reform" is a straw man.

Reformers are not commonly former teachers or principals. They're more frequently people who have never attempted to inspire a youthful audience all day, every day for months, let alone years.

Also, throughout my career, I couldn't help noticing that most reforms involved "fixing" the teachers, insisting on higher benchmarks and additional coursework, none of which had ever been proven to enhance the quality of instruction. Although continuing to stay current is certainly necessary, I couldn't help wondering why educational reform didn't extend to improving the attitudes of our clientele. (Of course that would require revamping an entire society.)

So how do you survive all the externally imposed "solutions" lobbed at you like tennis balls without turning cynical? By becoming to some degree an impartial observer. If you stay in this profession long enough (and I hope you do), you'll observe the same or at least similar philosophies rolling around a second, perhaps even a third time.

Example: memorization and objective testing were really hot in the 1950s. (When I was in school, if a lesson happened to be intriguing, it was probably an accident.) Then came the 1960s, with an abrupt turn. The emphasis became relevance, telling it like it is, personal freedom, and teaching the "whole" child.

Guess where we are now (again). And guess where we're probably headed—but not anytime soon. Granted, what was missing in the 1950s was teacher accountability. But its present form is accountability run amok, holding one person (teacher) accountable for the independent actions of another (student). In other words, tweaking only one half of the equation.

Teachers are not solely responsible for all educational outcomes. This is supposed to be a team effort—yet we still blame only one (and the same) player when anyone falls short.

Just wait—and watch. If you can rise above it, the sudden rush to embrace whatever's new or simple will be far more entertaining than anything you'll ever see on TV.

# Despite the current testing frenzy, you'll always be teaching people, not subjects.

Although I recognize that proficiency testing is a very necessary part of measuring what's being learned, I still call the current movement a frenzy—and as such, it has the potential for enormous abuse and therefore damage. That also means there's a very good chance that twenty years down the pike we'll all be shaking our heads and asking, "What were we thinking?"

Testing beyond basic literacy skills and rudimentary knowledge overlooks the fact that much of learning is retroactive. Most kids don't retain what's taught until they find a way to incorporate it into their lives. Only when it becomes relevant does the light dawn. The same person who was bored stiff in geography class begins to travel in his late twenties and suddenly can't buy enough maps. The same person who slept through geometry decides to major in architecture and whips through a year's worth of high school material in just forty-five minutes.

In a few isolated cases, our requirements verge on the absurd. Take reading selections. How can any high school kid understand Willy Loman's midlife crisis in *Death of a Salesman*? Thirty years later, though, it will hit him right in the gut.

Also, due to learning differences, many talented people don't test well. And although every child who graduates from high school should certainly have a basic grasp of math, reading, writing, history, science, government, and critical thinking skills, we've progressed far beyond that point. Some of these tests have become tools with which to browbeat students, teachers, or both—and creative, fun types of lessons could become relics of the past. Your unit on the Inuit probably won't allow for a gourmet chef's visit and a taste of real whale blubber—not when there's yet another proficiency exam next week. Too bad. The kids would still get excited decades later whenever they talked about that blubber.

So I'm a great believer in the power of sandwiching. You may be required to devote most of your time to the bread—the material that's likely to be tested. But you can do it briskly, with energy, sudden shouts, foreign accents, movie star impersonations . . . you get the idea. Move it along. And then reserve your final ten minutes to include your sandwich fillings, in this case a tray of blubber, so everyone gets a taste.

# The feds, however, have turned up the heat.

No Child Left Behind. You know it well. As if teaching weren't already stressful enough, you are now under tremendous pressure to make certain that all your students pass their proficiency tests. All. (Your tired, your poor, your huddled masses yearning to breathe free . . . ) Okay, districts are allowed to exempt a small percentage of developmentally disabled students, but not always as many as are enrolled. And I've heard stories about kids being in this country for mere weeks, still unable to speak English, yet being expected to perform at grade level.

What's more, you, your school, and your district are evaluated and labeled according to those test results.

Like so many ideas, this one sounded great in its original concept. Of course no student should be promoted until he's mastered the required material. Of course it's the school's responsibility to make sure that happens. But that's also part of the problem—as always, schools being forced to absorb *all* responsibility, regardless of the student's ability level, background, motivation, respect for authority, or desire to learn.

Because during my last ten years I specialized in vocational students, I saw many future carpenters, welders, auto mechanics, and machine trades workers beaten to an emotional pulp by the prospect of more and more proficiency testing on subjects they'd likely never need for their careers. Now, years later, I'm hearing about increased dropout rates—if these kids can't possibly win, they figure, then why would they want to play the game? And the greatest tragedy is that every dedicated teacher wants to turn his or her students on not just to knowledge but to learning. To make each person a lifelong seeker of new insights. For many students like mine, though, just the opposite is happening.

Did public education need to change? Were some teachers leaning back, hiding behind the sports pages while the kids worked on math problems at their seats? Of course. But the pendulum has swung so far in the opposite direction toward classrooms driven by standardized testing that I wonder how much longer I'd have been able to spare the time to discuss Lady Macbeth's wily tricks against her husband and then demonstrate similar manipulation through comical role playing with a boy in my class—in other words, bring Shakespeare to vibrant life for a vocational English class.

The most inspiring lessons, the ones remembered forever, will never come from a workbook or be reflected on a proficiency test. Keep that in mind as you prepare for yet another. It may provide some consolation.

# There's already an intriguing reform idea out there.

If we really want outstanding teachers to become the norm, says Malcolm Gladwell, author of *The Tipping Point* and *Outliers*, then we need to stop looking at their college-level GPAs and stop requiring hideously expensive and time-consuming advanced degrees.

Instead, open the floodgates and let in anyone who wants to give teaching a try. The reason: no one can predict, no matter what kind of measurement is used, who will become a creative, inspirational genius. "No one knows," Gladwell says, "what a person with the potential to be a great teacher looks like"—until he or she is observed inside a classroom, that is, working with kids. And the right qualities show up super-early. Within weeks, or even days. There are "competencies" that can be easily spotted: a regard for the student's perspective; the ability to give high-quality feedback, where there's a back-and-forth exchange to reach a deeper understanding; and "with-itness," which means knowing what's going on in every corner of the room and inside every child's head.

Retain the good guys, Gladwell adds. Let them teach up a storm for decades—but pay them the salaries they deserve. That last variable (higher pay) might just attract the larger number of star performers we need to change the face of American education.

How many of them, I wonder, are currently hiding in banking, medicine, real estate sales, psychology, motivational speaking, or law—but are unwilling to earn a mere $35,000 per year for a seventy-hour workweek? For more on this, read the section of *Outliers* where Gladwell compares teachers to quarterbacks.

Is it possible that our unwillingness to pay well for our best and brightest, who might come to us from a variety of fields, is all that's standing in the way of having universally superb schools?

# If you're a teacher who's really suffering, it could be due to bad placement.

I began my career by teaching ninth graders, and as the saying goes, somebody up there really, really liked me. I'd had no way of knowing beforehand that it would be the ideal level for me at that point in my life—the kids weren't too young or too old, but just right. Ten years later, once I'd put on a smidgen of age and experience, I was more than ready to transfer to high school. But somewhere in between those two points, I was assigned a class of seventh graders.

They were sweet, and I enjoyed them, but it wasn't a level that sparked my true passion—or even my best performance.

Now, looking back, I realize that too many young teachers who bite the dust might have done better with a simple switch in grade level. Can one or two years really make that much difference? Yes. If I'd tried to teach juniors and seniors at age twenty-one, they would have eaten me for lunch. I could easily have become another teaching casualty.

So I'm wondering if a first-year teacher who's lying awake at night, seriously questioning his or her career choice, shouldn't take a couple of professional days to travel the district and observe a variety of levels—and see if one of them doesn't set his or her heart racing.

> "Tell me and I'll forget. Show me, and I may not remember. Involve me, and I'll understand."
> **—NATIVE AMERICAN PROVERB**

# Understand the faculty "family."

Think of it as a scene from *Leave It to Beaver*. There's Pop, the authoritarian principal—even if he is a she. There's Mom, the assistant or dean, who's friendlier, more hands-on, more likely to visit your classroom between bells just to chat. There's Wally, the kid (teacher) who always does what he's told. There's the Beaver, who has good intentions but always seems to mess up. Then there's Eddie Haskell, the suck-up who's thought to be a good worker by higher-ups, but all the kids (teachers) know he's really a dorky con artist. And there's Lumpy, who's just plain dull and doesn't even realize it. Have some fun with this spotting of archetypes. There's a reason they crop up so often in all types of literature, ranging from fables to sitcoms.

# The teachers' lounge may or may not be a warm, fuzzy environment.

Teachers rarely have anyone to whom they can vent their frustrations—so they erupt to each other, and usually during their unassigned periods in the lounge. You'll learn a lot about faculty politics (not to mention gossip), but you'll also run the risk of becoming mired in a gloomy environment. Unfortunately, it can become addictive, sort of like a soap opera where everyone's drowning in dysfunction. This varies from school to school, of course, but be wary. If you find yourself regularly going back to class in a foul mood, you might want to think about limiting your visits.

> "Turn your wounds into wisdom.
> **—OPRAH WINFREY**

Some teachers voice their worries about feeling disconnected if they stay away—a valid concern. But I believe that new teachers should do far more listening than talking. That's not due to a need to "remember your place," but because much of what you say can be misconstrued. Hearing any overt criticism of a fellow teacher or administrator, for example, should result in your becoming totally immersed in those quizzes you're grading.

# Don't expect everyone on the faculty to be your cheering section.

You've just put together an eye-catching bulletin board, or you've just completed a dynamic lesson that had your kids jumping out of their seats. You're on cloud nine. You rush next door to share your excitement with Mrs. Green, a veteran teacher whose insights and experiences you value. But a strange thing happens. The more you talk and wave your arms and grin, the less interested Mrs. Green seems. Soon her deadpan expression is so deflating that you leave, feeling completely bummed. What's going on?

You threatened her, that's what. Your youthful enthusiasm reminds her too much of what she once had.

Young teachers, by virtue of their limitless energy, can tap-dance circles around most of us oldsters. That's not to say that we aren't masters at what we do; many of us are. But you probably won't find us skipping down the hall and singing on the days that everything goes right.

Also, when you make suggestions during teachers' meetings, you may even hear caustic remarks like "Yeah, we tried that eight years ago; it didn't work" or "Your idealism won't last; you'll change once you get hit with a solid dose of reality. We all do." (Not necessarily, but the sourpusses would like you to think so.)

Choose your boosters carefully. Avoid the grumblers and the snivelers; look instead for serene sages whose eyes still sparkle and who talk about their students (and their profession) with genuine pleasure. Don't overlook administrators; despite the sometimes bad press about their being too removed from the student body, they can be equally devoted. And remember: you aren't doing anything wrong by getting excited about your job.

# Zero tolerance isn't as nutty as it sounds.

Our news media love stories about school districts that outlaw carrying knives and then expel some poor little first grader whose mother placed a plastic one inside his lunch box. Makes us look like morons.

What they never tell the reading public is that such expulsions are nearly always overturned. Administrators count on parents in such cases to file grievances. Zero tolerance is in place to ensure that the seventeen-year-old who hides a butcher blade inside his backpack with the intention of carving up his former girlfriend's new boyfriend after gym class really can be expelled, according to predetermined, clearly stated rules.

These days everyone considers himself an exceptional case. Everyone expects to be cut a break. So zero tolerance makes it possible to make a punishment stick when the situation calls for it.

But you won't find that in any news headline. It's not outrageous, freaky, or sexy enough. It's just plain common sense.

# Don't hate the union because it's powerful.

Without it we'd all still be making $2,500 per year. Teachers used to board with parents, sleeping on someone's cot for a month or so, then shuffling along to stay with the next family in the village. Women lost their jobs when they married. Boards fired instructors who discussed topics against their personal politics. I'm not kidding.

The current horror stories you hear about teachers' unions, such as demanding that class sizes be limited to twenty, come from the old days when some teachers endured groups of fifty with no end in sight and no additional compensation. "Unreasonable" demands on one side generally come from a long, sorry history of unreasonable expectations on the other.

# You'll probably dislike being evaluated.

Teaching is far more art than science, and we're all a little fearful that our evaluator won't quite "get" it. Should an administrator whose background is in, say, math be rating a teacher of literature or music? Probably not. But that's often the way the system works. So help him or her out. Furnish a handout beforehand (or the next day if it's a surprise visit) explaining your aims, motives, techniques, and follow-ups. And try to keep an open mind. If there's magic taking place, if the kids are excited and everyone's clamoring to be heard, believe me, your evaluator will pick up on it.

Also, prepare to be surprised. For years I considered my strongest suit to be friendly relationships with my students—until one day an observant assistant principal informed me that my incredible knowledge of subject matter left everything, even my warmth, in the dust. Who knew? Funny how that sort of thing can creep up on you over the years.

This is emblematic, I think, of the teaching profession as a whole. You'll work hard all of your professional career to become an inspiration. And what your students will recall best will always be the traits, actions, and one-liners you didn't plan and can barely remember. What an evaluator picks up by watching and listening may be a compelling draw you weren't even aware that you had.

# Teachers' meetings and in-service days could use an overhaul.

Most have prescribed agendas—a series of announcements, or guest speakers whose ideas may or may not be relevant and useful. For some reason, the notion of giving teachers unstructured time still makes some administrators shudder. Perhaps they're afraid we might (gasp) leave the building.

In reality, we're all a little giddy at the prospect of enjoying lunch in a restaurant where the utensils aren't made of plastic.

But seriously . . . maybe sitting around in a group, comparing notes on what we perceive as our own unique challenges might result in others nodding in recognition and suggesting some excellent remedies. Districts already instituting what they call professional learning communities have found that mutual sharing and support are more than worth the extra investment of time.

# Compulsory education may have outlived its usefulness.

I know, I know. Total blasphemy. Everyone needs a basic education and a high school diploma in order to survive.

But by the time a child reaches about age fifteen, he has pretty well made up his mind how seriously he's going to take that enterprise. I encountered many (many, many) "students" who'd simply closed down shop and sat all day with their arms folded, refusing to open a book or turn in a paper.

Sometimes it was a form of passive aggression—"I'll show up, but you can't make me work." (They were right; I couldn't.) In other cases, as soon as they were legally able, they quit school. All my efforts to motivate and encourage fell on deaf ears.

Were they sorry later? Of course they were. But no one could have told them that at a time when they still, as the saying goes, knew everything. And I'm not sure my resources were always well spent trying to convince them to stay. What was truly ironic was that six years later, they'd come back and boast that they'd earned their GEDs and were now enrolled in community college.

I finally reached the conclusion that some kids needed to experience the harshness of the real working world before they realized what a good deal high school was. Meanwhile, my awareness recalled that classic line from my grandfather's day: you can lead a horse to water, but you can't make him drink. (We teachers are required to force a lot of nonthirsty kids to drink.)

Investing energy in those who simply aren't interested becomes a very frustrating drain. Sort of like marketing shiny new tennis rackets to people who don't play. Education isn't exactly a tennis racket; it's not something one can choose not to purchase. But people do so in their own time and with their own consent. Sometimes that's not until age twenty-four.

> " I truly believe that education is the solution to most of this country's problems. Give good teachers a small enough group of kids to work with, and we can get the majority of them drug-free, alcohol-free, full of values and respect and mentally healthy . . . then what would we need prisons for? "
> — **JOHN GODAR**

What can you do in the meantime? Reinforce the importance of a high school or college diploma by citing the stats on increased lifetime earning potentials. Associate's degree holders earn between $7,300 and $9,900 more annually than high school graduates; bachelor's degree holders earn between $13,900 and $22,900 more.* Multiply each figure by forty to see what the career total looks like. Then accept the fact that everyone has the right to make a bad choice—but that her choice needn't be permanent. In the majority of cases, this one won't be. Bide your time.

There's no definitive answer here. Except perhaps what I suggest on the next page . . . that similar results might be realized within a shorter time frame.

*Source: From http://www.collegeboard.com/prod_downloads/press/cost06/education_pays_06.pdf, accessed June 5, 2009

# Public schooling needn't last twelve years.

I've always believed that if we operated more efficiently, we could probably wrap things up in ten. Beginning in about eighth or ninth grade (perhaps earlier in cases of true child prodigies, but we'd need to be watchful of social unreadiness), we might offer our kids the option of a fast track, where they do most of their work independently. Give selected teachers office hours, like at universities, with entire classes meeting only twice each week. Students would need to assume total responsibility for getting assignments in on time and checking with teachers whenever they needed help.

No assemblies, no fire drills, no drama clubs, no attendance monitoring, no study halls, no election of class officers. Would that work immediately for everyone? No. Would it work better in the long run than what we have now? In time, yes.

Condensing grades one through seven would be far more difficult, because there's still so much physical, emotional, and social growth going on. Some authorities suggest longer school days and longer school years. Perhaps seasonal three-week breaks would work better—and eliminate spending the first month each fall reviewing what's been forgotten over the summer.

What we have right now is a gargantuan machine, dedicated not only to education in small nuggets but also to an entire social structure continually required to transport, feed, medicate, assess, and evaluate. And to house young people, keeping them well out of the way of the adult business world until they're old enough to join it.

It's a machine, therefore, that chugs along slowly, consuming vast amounts of time, energy—and money. As financial crises and proficiency demands increase, what we'll eventually need to address is whether or not we want to continue moving at that pace, or come up with a much different plan.

Throughout your entire career, you'll be hearing from multiple fronts (parents, administrators, politicians, and taxpayers), many of whom will claim to have the ultimate answers to how schools should be run. It's easy to become distracted and confused.

But you as a teacher can claim a kind of insight that no one else has. You are with your students for at least an hour every single day. You know how they think, how they behave, how they learn. You know what works best—for them and for you.

# Some things you'll never grow accustomed to.

Like what I used to call the 5:30 A.M. body slam. From my first day of teaching in 1968 to my last in 1999, my frame never grew accustomed to the shock of hearing the alarm go off before dawn. There were many days, in fact, when I fell back asleep while standing under the shower spray.

Whoever decided that the world should revolve around morning people, anyway? Expecting a teacher to be vibrant and bouncy at 7:00 A.M. every day without exception is, in my mind, a crime against humanity.

And each time I read a new report stating that teenagers' internal clocks aren't set for early learning either, I can't help wondering why we go on, decade after decade, torturing so many.

> "Seven-thirty in the morning. It was the earliest I had arrived at work since I had been discharged from the army."
> **—STUART B. PALONSKY**

# Survival is indeed for the fittest—and that's you.

Although the loneliness and isolation of this profession are definite drawbacks, there's a cool contradiction worth noting: your students will drain and exhaust you—but they will also engage and energize you.

I can't think of anyplace else where one person has the privilege of constant intellectual interaction with others of so many diverse backgrounds, frameworks, temperaments, and personalities. Will some of their freely offered opinions and remarks horrify you? Yes. Will others give you a fresh perspective, perhaps even illuminate and fast-track your own evolution? Yes again.

Remember, the world revolves around the young. We adults may make the rules, but they test, blur, and tweak them. We may market the clothing, the cars, and the electronics, but they decide whether or not those offerings are hip enough to buy.

Seeing our society through their eyes will keep you thinking like a young person. You're less likely to fall prey to uttering the dreaded line, "Back in my day . . ." You already understand that it isn't your day; it's theirs. But your wisdom and influence still color their world, just as their brash enthusiasm colors yours.

A warning: don't expect diplomacy or tact. Try not to get your feelings hurt when their assessments can be as off-putting as this: "Oh. You got your hair cut. I don't like it."

At the same time, it usually makes sense to listen. One former student who otherwise enjoyed my company remarked one day, "You need to stop complaining about the weather. It makes you sound old." Appalled, I stopped immediately.

To teach—and to keep learning—is to remain youthful forever.

# 3

# Finding Your Teacher Persona

*I had to carefully choose from my arsenal. Too weak would not be heard. Too strong would make students laugh.*

**—Gary Rubenstein**

# Create and cultivate a commanding presence.

Why does Mr. A have almost no discipline problems, but Mr. B has dozens of them? Easy. Mr. B is a wimp.

Yes, it truly is that simple. Kids have terrific radar. They know whom they can ride like a mule and who will toss them off onto the ground. You hardly need to say a word.

It's difficult to define a commanding presence—but it's incredibly easy to spot one. Oprah Winfrey has it. Robin Williams has it. Katie Couric has it. Larry King has it. You may not like any of these people, but you're unlikely to tangle with them one-on-one. They could sweep the floor with you—in fact, the whole parking lot—and possibly hit you with a verbal zinger that would take you decades to get over. The odd thing is they rarely need to do so, because few people they encounter are foolish enough to test them.

Once, long ago, an *Oprah* guest made so many silly declarations that he became the target of constant laughter. He turned to Ms. Winfrey and demanded, "Get control of your audience!" Quick as a shot, Lady O came back with, "I run this show, not you." Spectators erupted into wild applause.

So here are some clues: people with presence cannot be intimidated. They're comfortable with their particular brand of authority, whatever that may be. (As you may have already gathered, mine was unbelievably laid-back.) They also don't try to hide their talents. They're happy to take center stage—yet they willingly share the spotlight. And most surprising: they aren't generally drill sergeants. They more often begin by coming from kindness.

> " I thought it would be a good idea if my students believed my hands were registered lethal weapons. "
>
> **—LOUANNE JOHNSON**

While we're on the subject, let me tell you a secret: the worst screamers who refuse to make exceptions for anyone, regardless of the circumstances, are really scared. Scared that someone will find out they're actually wimps.

So how do you avoid wimpdom and cultivate presence? Read on.

# Make an entrance.

You stand at your door between classes and greet everyone with enthusiasm—even your student who made the unflattering remark yesterday about your spouse (I'm kidding, sort of). When the bell rings, you stride with purpose into the room. Don't saunter, slouch, or meander. You might sit down for a moment to take attendance, but once you're finished, you rise and approach the class, their signal that it's time to begin.

> The most precious gift we can offer others is our presence. When mindfulness embraces those we love, they will bloom like flowers.
> —THICH NHAT HANH

# Never shout over a class; instead wait for them to quiet down.

Oh, sure, you say; that'll probably take half the period.

No, it won't. Not if you're patient. Each day it will take less and less time, and soon it will be three seconds.

Somewhere around year twenty, with my more sociable groups, I started saying simply, "I will wait for you." For some reason my students thought that was cute, and it became a trademark: "She will wait for us. She is waiting for *you*, John." Giggles all around—and then I could begin.

I hope I don't need to add that I wasn't wearing a prune face. I wasn't glaring, all cloaked in my schoolmarmish armor. I was smiling, as if we had lots of intriguing stuff to do that day. And we did.

Please don't underestimate the enormous power of this single act of waiting. Unfortunately I can't take total credit; I stole it from a high school girl in 1978, a student council president addressing an all-school assembly. She stood at a podium and waited for the entire group, some one thousand people, to get quiet before she spoke. It took at least five minutes, and it seemed more like an hour. But gradually we could all hear, "Shhh! Shhh!" from various sections of the gym—and suddenly there was total silence.

Every teacher in the place was slack jawed, including me.

Contrast that with the many times I've walked past an open-doored classroom and observed a colleague "teaching" a lesson over the din of his chattering class. Occasionally I'd hear, "Will you please quiet down?"

But when the class continued to talk, the teacher merely continued with his lesson.

Don't be a wimp. It's definitely worth the initial investment of time to train your classes to listen up the moment your demeanor declares that instruction is about to start.

# Cultivate a clear, commanding voice.

It will be loud enough for everyone to hear, but not raised in anger. There's a huge difference. It will be expressive, not droning. It will not be filled with "um" and "uh" and "you know" and "like." It will not contain buffers like "sort of" and "kind of" and "I was thinking maybe we should . . ." Although you may never completely eradicate such annoying stoppers, you can significantly reduce their use. Try never to diminish or disqualify yourself through your own speech.

Also, remember that the more someone talks, the less he or she is listened to. (Remember your last teachers' meeting?) Get the instruction portion of your lesson over with, so the kids can get to work. (And don't repeat yourself three times.) Or else create a discussion springboard, and then let your students carry it as much as possible.

Finally, learn the incredible power of silence. If somebody is spinning a deceitful web to get out of trouble, just fix him with an unwavering stare. Then issue a simple request: "Run past me again why you were rummaging through that locked cabinet—and why my key is missing."

The same goes if someone starts talking while you're giving instructions. Stop in midsentence, stare, and raise a questioning eyebrow, as if you believe the student is confused. Perhaps you say, "Pete? Something?" Then when he shakes his head, go on as if nothing happened.

When dealing with a single student at her desk, don't raise your voice; lower it. "Would you please put that iPod away?" Amazingly, the entire class will suddenly turn stone silent. You got their attention. By whispering.

# Take advantage of your most powerful time window—the first day of school.

Even the worst troublemakers are reticent on the first day. They're wary; they're defensive; they're sizing you up. If you make a great first impression, they might just decide you're not worth hassling. Hey, it happens!

Also, no matter how much difficulty a kid has caused in the past, every fall feels like a fresh start. Maybe this year will be different. You know how you can tell? By 8:00 A.M. on that first day, the temperature has already risen to eighty-five degrees—but a boy in the third row is wearing a long-sleeved sweater! Why? Because it's new, and he wants to look nice. This seemingly foolish clothing choice looked much different to me once I learned to read it correctly.

Don't dash any kid's hopes by instantly becoming a drill sergeant. Don't begin the year with a list of "thou shalt nots."

Of course you'll eventually hand out a list of expectations (please don't call them rules), with extra copies readily available for those who lose them (they will)—but that first day should be used for only one purpose: getting everyone excited about the coming year. Present a verbal outline of the cool, interesting topics you plan to pursue.

Latecomers who miss your opening remarks will still pick up the electric atmosphere.

# Take yourself out of the authority loop; eliminate all vestiges of Me Against You.

This is essential. First of all, if you're enjoying your drill sergeant role too much, then you're in the wrong business. I've always been deeply suspicious of teachers who are especially eager to "show those little twerps who's boss."

Never put yourself in the position of Supreme Being. You are not infallible. Once, following a spelling quiz, I found what looked like a crib sheet inside the desk of one of my best students. Full of righteous teacher indignation, I confronted her at the doorway. She calmly explained that she'd used it to review, then right before the quiz began, she'd tucked it far into her desk. She was calm, unruffled. Not the least bit belligerent.

I paused and took a deep breath. In my heart and my gut I knew she was telling the truth. So I sent the girl on her way. Thank goodness. To this day, thirty-five years later, I'm still relieved that I needed to be fair more than I needed to be justified.

# Don't feel the need to answer every complaint. Commiserate, commiserate, commiserate!

This is the best way to stay out of the loop. A kid enters your room out of breath but grousing about the length of the lunch line, how there's never anything good to eat, and how he's not even allowed to stop at his locker.

The authoritarian response: "So you think life is a bed of roses? You expect everything to run on your timetable? Get used to it, kiddo: life isn't fair, and it never will be! Your responsibility is still to get to my class on time!"

Your better response: "Oh, I know! Don't you just hate that?"

A kid forgets his research paper on the day it's due. He's declaring that it wasn't his fault; his mother didn't place it on the kitchen table.

The authoritarian response: "Is it your mother's job to make sure you're wearing clean underwear and your lunch is packed? Why don't you just grow up?"

Your better response: "Don't you hate it when you forget things? Well, at least this is a mistake you'll make only one time."

# Don't feel the need to resolve every problem.

The kid who forgot his research paper already knows he'll need to turn it in the next morning and receive a lower grade. You don't need to rub his nose in it by stating the obvious. If he starts asking, "But why can't I . . . ?" you smile, give his shoulder an affectionate squeeze and reply, "Because then you won't remember the lesson about needing to get organized." Then you turn to speak to someone else. Don't get snared into a public debate.

# Become a broken record.

If the student gets snarly and won't let an issue go, repeat the same line: "You won't remember the lesson." (Note that this is light years away from "I need to teach you a lesson." The second makes you a drill sergeant. The first makes you a compassionate sage.) Say it again as often as necessary. This works especially well with elementary students who are still struggling with impulse control. Most are well aware that they sometimes act without thinking, and a nonjudgmental reminder to think first should be received with grace.

In a worst-case scenario, you may need to request quietly that the two of you discuss the matter further after school. To save face in front of his peers, the kid may huff, "We sure will."

But I'll bet you ten dollars he won't show up.

And on the following day, when he shoves his paper at you, just smile and say, "Thank you." No speeches, no reprimands. No need.

# Your body language speaks volumes.

Your students will sense whether or not you really care, or if you're in it for, as people say, the money. But even if there's no question about your commitment, students will continually inquire and find ways to test you. So go ahead: be shameless in your open declarations of love. Even when you're exasperated, you'll need to preface your sternness with, "You guys know I adore you, but . . ." It may sound corny to you, but even high school seniors will lap it up.

Meanwhile, check all your biases at the door. You'll receive your fair share of stunning surprises. That morose boy in the third row will turn out to be a budding artistic genius whose potential has long gone unrecognized. The girl wearing the ripped, ragged jeans will turn out to be the granddaughter of your town's most generous philanthropist. Every time you make an assumption, fate has an interesting way of showing you a flip side.

As for openly voicing frustrations about your profession in class, tread lightly here. Kids take everything personally. Take a moment to remind your class that the only teachers who aren't at least a little angry about how schools are run are those who've ceased to care.

# Don't take hostility too personally.

Chances are good that it's not even about you. Learn to distinguish between kids who are mad about something you did and just plain mad about everything.

With middle and high school students, remember that you're dealing with an age group that is discovering, perhaps for the first time, that even when you work hard and delay gratification, life may still not give you what you want. Other people make the rules, but you have to follow them. The government confiscates a huge percentage of your hard-earned money to fund causes you don't believe in. Somebody else will always be richer, faster, smarter, and better looking.

Worst of all, the only thing they can do about it is get angry, often without understanding why.

# Light up when a kid enters your room or study hall.

Act delighted to see everyone. Always greet him or her with heartfelt enthusiasm. Sounds crazy? Well, think about how many kids never see that light in anyone's eyes. Think about how good you feel whenever someone is thrilled to see you.

# Talk less, teach more.

This is much harder than it sounds. It involves waiting for a student to think through his or her response. It involves resisting the impulse to supply every answer and fill every silence. It involves letting a concept sink in for a moment before lobbing a fourth, fifth, and sixth insight. It involves asking more multilayered questions than those that require only one-word answers, more examination and analysis than simple solutions.

And there's currently so much pressure to hurry through every lesson and "cover" all of the required material.

Perhaps you'll feel better if I admit that encouraging your students to delve deeper rather than shooting from the hip is something that few of us ever master. It requires an almost genius-level alertness—to whatever is going on in the moment, what everyone's reaction is likely to be within the next thirty seconds, how you should respond to elicit more participation, and where you'd like the discussion to wind up at the period's end.

Keep trying. You'll get better and better.

# Lean forward during a student's response to a class discussion.

It means you're really listening instead of just waiting so you can return to being such a know-it-all. Each time one of my students contradicted one of my "insights" with a well-reasoned reply, I broke into an elated grin. It meant that he or she was thinking faster than I was. How cool was that?

> It is the province of knowledge to speak and it is the privilege of wisdom to listen.
> **—OLIVER WENDELL HOLMES**

> Know how to listen, and you will profit even from those who talk badly.
> **—PLUTARCH**

# Never tell your class how difficult an assignment is.

Tell them it's challenging. Tell them it's invigorating. Tell them you'll be proud of them once they complete it.

Also, speak in terms of shortcuts. Say, for example, "You can save yourself a lot of grief if you . . . [start early, get the research out of the way first, interview a neighbor or family member about this current event]."

Many projects and assignments already look intimidating enough. Don't add to the burden by making them look darn near impossible. If you make it a rule to cut to the chase rather than wasting your students' time, you will endear yourself far more than you realize.

# Never offer the kind of help that disempowers.

The more you do for someone, the less he does for himself. It's called learned helplessness.

Remember that old saw about teaching someone to fish?

> "Give a man a fish, and you feed him for a day. Teach him how to fish, and you feed him for a lifetime."
> —**LAO TZU**

Offer a boost, not a bailout. When a student claims not to understand an assignment, you'll be tempted to show him in detail how to get started—and suddenly, before you know it, the task is completed, but you've done most of the work. So give him just three minutes. Ask lots of questions. Then stop. Hand the paper back. Smile.

# Sprinkle small, tantalizing tidbits.

There comes a time when we all want to hear other people's perceptions. But most children and teens aren't there yet. So be a bit hesitant about spilling your own guts, wisdom, and experience. Tease them instead: "Back in college, I worked as a garbage collector, and some homeless guy in an alley said the wisest thing I've ever heard from anyone."

Then wait. See if they beg for more. If not, move on.

The first time you hear a kid ask, "What do you mean by that?" give yourself a silent cheer. In time, if you play your cards right, you'll become one of those select few adults whom young people genuinely respect and want to listen to. There may well be no higher compliment.

> " The mediocre teacher tells. The good teacher explains. The superior teacher demonstrates. The great teacher inspires. "
>
> **—WILLIAM ARTHUR WARD**

# Be awed by the concept of universal education.

Think about how many societies (and families) worldwide deny the right of an education to certain groups of people—most commonly females. Then consider the strength of those that attempt to offer it to everyone.

Educating children, after all, guarantees that they will grow up to question the ways that their families, their communities, and their governments do things—and then criticize the always imperfect results. It takes immense courage, therefore, to accept that our kids, because we teach them to think for themselves, will likely decide that everything we've done thus far is wrong!

Yet we continue to arm them lovingly with all we know, and then hope that they will someday know more and do better.

Staggering, isn't it? We no longer question education's value; we're just seeking better ways to sweep more people into the net, even those who disdain it.

# Remember what it was like to be a seventh grader.

All raging hormones, no common sense, no coping skills, constantly evaluated and criticized by adults during the most vulnerable, most insecure time of your life. Wanting desperately to be liked and admired by your friends, but with no idea how to get there. Knowing that you will eventually need to find a job that will support you and perhaps also a young family—when right now you can't even imagine earning enough to keep gas in the tank.

Memories coming back? I hope so. Childhood and adolescence are truly no picnic. Be gentle.

> "Young people are in a condition like permanent intoxication, because youth is sweet and they are growing."
>
> **—ARISTOTLE**

# 4

..............................................................

# Money and Other Compensations

> *Teacher? I never dreamed I could rise so high in the world.*
> —**Frank McCourt**

# Salaries aren't as bad as they used to be, but they still have a way to go.

I signed my first teaching contract in 1968 for $5,600. My fellow college graduates in other fields were beginning their careers at around $8,000 or $9,000. Back then I shrugged at the disparity; it wasn't enough to make me turn away from a field I had already grown to love.

Twenty years later, when my friends in business and industry were earning two to three times what I was making, I was far less philosophical.

> "America believes in education: the average professor earns more money in a year than a professional athlete earns in a whole week."
> **—EVAN ESAR**

During the mid-1980s, I knew a man whose college GPA had been way below average, far below mine. Yet after eighteen years in management he proudly declared that he'd now be able to "coast" until retirement. His salary? $62,000. Mine? $16,000. And I was far from coasting, even on a slow day.

My dedication was still strong, but it wasn't as if my grocer and utility companies were giving me any discounts. How did I finally reconcile this? By realizing that we all make our own choices for our own reasons. Granted, I'd made them when I was still too young to understand the impact. But no one ever becomes a teacher expecting to get rich.

# Salaries still differ radically, not only from state to state but from district to district.

The disparity within a thirty-five-mile radius, depending on property values, can be as much as $10,000—for the very same job assignment, years of training, experience, and degree of talent. My advice to you? Shop around. And then keep on shopping. Some better-paying districts actually prefer to hire teachers with three to five years of experience.

Using real estate taxes to fund public education has long been declared unconstitutional, but so far no one seems especially eager to change anything. Deep down, we Americans don't have the political will, or whatever it takes, to fund an educational system that doesn't reinforce our class distinctions. No rich guy wants to pay for some poor kid's schooling. And no lawmaker wants to force him. That's why the same foolish system endures, decade after decade.

# Your workload (and hence your hourly rate) will also vary according to your subject matter—and your degree of dedication.

Unless you're a coach, if you teach physical education, your days will all end precisely at dismissal time, 2:45 P.M. If you teach English, you can count on adding a minimum of fifteen additional hours to your workweek. All unpaid. If you teach math or history, your expenditure of energy will fall somewhere in between.

Adding to the inequity, if you're a guidance counselor or a vocational instructor, you're likely to receive an extended time contract—which amounts to between two and four weeks that you'll report for duty before the beginning and after the end of each school year. For which you are also paid extra. It's designed to compensate you for your additional preparation and wrap-up time.

If you teach English, math, or history, you're still expected to prepare and wrap up, of course. On your own time. Which means you don't get paid for it.

The reason? Simple. Counseling and vocational programs are relatively recent developments in public education; hence those perks were negotiated for and agreed to by school boards. Also, at least some of the costs are picked up by state or federal funding. English, math, and history classes, in contrast, were all born during an era when it would have been unthinkable for teachers to negotiate for much of anything. They were just grateful to have jobs.

For elementary school teachers, the workload doesn't differ as wildly among grade levels as much as it does through the dedication of individual teachers—which is true at all levels. There will always be a few who perform on a minimal plane, combined with many, many more who put in hundreds of additional hours each year. What's more, most of those hours will be invisible. No one will know the difference except the teacher herself. And occasionally a few observant students.

Still, refusing to show up early or stay late, or waiting until school starts to get things organized will amount to shooting yourself in the foot. You'll spend the entire semester feeling as if you're running two weeks behind. And you will be.

# The toughest assignments often pay the least.

Ironic, isn't it? The affluent suburbs, where students are more likely to have interested parents and home computers, nearly always pay their teachers better than inner-city or rural districts, where we're dealing with less home support and more emotional baggage than we can shake a stick at. The reason, of course, is that involved parents are more likely to vote yes for school levies, which ultimately means more equitable raises.

But there really are more important things than money. Throughout your professional life, you'll never need to wonder whether or not you're contributing something to the betterment of the human race. You'll know it in your heart every single day. With all due respect, I'm not sure that marketing toothpaste or selling preowned cars carries the same psychic benefits.

> "Many of the snarly, bad-tempered teachers whom we remember were really nice people soured by years of anxiety and penny-pinching."
> **—GILBERT HIGHET**

And those really tough assignments? You'll see the results almost immediately. Kids without any advantages except dedicated teachers are amazingly great about saying thank you. Privileged kids too often see the help they receive as an entitlement. I began to notice this only after I was receiving huge verbal bouquets of sheepish gratitude from my at-risk students and weepy graduation-day hugs from their parents.

# Teaching summer school is a pretty decent deal—if you can stand the heat.

You're paid by the hour, and your students are forking over money for makeup classes from their own checking accounts (or at least their parents are), so they're likely to be reasonably motivated. On the down side, you'll give up all but three weeks of your mental health break. Also, if your building isn't air-conditioned, you'll be sweating in a sauna every day—and, to add insult to injury, buying your own electric fans.

Still, I took on the summer school stint for about eighteen years, and except for my soaking wet T-shirts, I pretty much enjoyed it. Classes ended at noon. Some very warm (no pun intended) teacher-student relationships developed. A terrific fringe benefit was coming back in the fall to several familiar faces and therefore an already well-forged classroom camaraderie. Those who weren't part of the summer school "team" fell into that friendly mode instantly.

# Night school and tutoring programs also make excellent part-time jobs—if you can muster the energy.

Try not to moonlight as a house painter. Or take too many continuing education classes during the school year. They'll turn you into a walking zombie. Night school teaching and one-on-one tutoring are another matter. There's often little or no additional travel, you're providing a critical service to your district, and you're helping kids graduate on time. Also, the individual conferences usually make discipline a nonissue. And the additional (hourly) wage buys your groceries.

There are worse ways to go.

> A little girl says to her teacher, "When I grow up, I want to be a teacher."
>
> "And for your night job?" replies the teacher.
>
> **—CARTOON FROM THE ILLINOIS EDUCATION ASSOCIATION'S NEA ADVOCATE**

# Don't vent to the kids about cash flows and mortgage payments; they really won't understand.

On the rare occasions that I articulated my frustrations about the teaching profession in general, my students would always respond, "Yes, but you get paid."

Ain't youth grand? In their view, the amount of money was irrelevant; having some coming in was the only consideration. Finally I caught on to their reasoning: to them, earned cash was something they got to spend as they wished. Electric bills, property taxes, leaky roofs, and refrigerators needing immediate replacement did not exist. Cars with killer stereo systems did. New shoes did.

We were addressing each other across the vast chasm of different life circumstances. It was a gulf that nothing would bridge—except time.

# Don't bother venting to friends and neighbors, either.

Periodically some guest editorialist decries how little teachers do these days and how overpaid they are. These are folks who, first, don't have enough of their own business to mind and, second, have never attempted our job. Even writer Anna Quindlen recently admitted that after she'd guest-lectured to three fifth-grade classes in a row, she was so exhausted that she wanted to go lie down for the rest of the day. (And the average teacher keeps on ticking for six to seven hours at a clip.)

Don't bellyache. No one will hear you. Everyone's still fixated on that mythical "three months' vacation" thing, not realizing that you've already crammed twelve months of work into nine, and then continued to slog away while everyone else is lounging on the beach. Console yourself by staying in touch with grateful parents who know how much you've changed their kids' lives. Pester them to remind you if necessary.

# Look for rewards in unconventional places.

They will come when you least expect them. Like when you run into a parent in a drugstore aisle, and she glows about the positive influence you've become in her child's life. Money is wonderful, and I'd never try to diminish its importance. But it's great to be reminded that the most lasting riches can't be bought at any price.

> "Try not to become a man of success but rather to become a man of value."
> —ALBERT EINSTEIN

# And speaking of unconventional...

If you don't attend your students' class reunions, then you're depriving yourself of one of teaching's greatest joys. Not only is it tremendous fun to see how everyone has turned out. As adults now, your "kids" are finally putting the pieces together, understanding why you always kept after them to try harder, be kinder, do better. Their defenses are down; they know how hard people work to provide for their families, so they're willing, even eager to proclaim how much they respect and admire you for helping them become successful.

Perhaps as I have, you'll even hear a few say, "The only reason I showed up tonight is because I thought you might be here."

Whew. Bring along plenty of tissues.

> "What's money? A man is a success if he gets up in the morning and goes to bed at night and in between does what he wants to do."
> **—BOB DYLAN**

# 5

## Nuts and Bolts

*The more that people have power over their own destiny, the harder and more creatively they work.*

**—William Glasser**

# Beg for chances to observe the most talented veterans.

As hard as it is to give up your only unassigned period, I strongly recommend asking your building's Teacher of the Year candidate if you can sit in on a class. You'll learn a great deal about physical presence, that recognizable quality every great teacher has. Listen carefully to how she introduces a topic, how she handles a wiseacre remark, why discipline is such a nonissue. And if by chance things don't go swimmingly, you'll learn something just as important—that even great teachers have off days. Also, there are some benefits to becoming a one-person fan club. You get to ask questions after school. You get to hear private words of wisdom. You get to visit again and again.

# You need a plan—but you may never quite get the timing right.

Each lesson requires a beginning, a middle, and an end; a pupil performance objective; and an evaluation. You need some way of figuring out whether or not you were effective in terms of holding attention; whether the lesson is part active, part passive (with the emphasis on active); and whether the kids actually learned anything new. Great educational moments rarely come about by accident; they take as much planning as D-Day.

Unfortunately, the whole thing can blow apart at the last minute, with the point entirely lost, because of a fire alarm, an unexpected PA announcement, or somebody falling out of his chair. And don't even ask what happens if a wasp buzzes into your room.

# Think outside the (text) box.

I never met a teacher's manual I didn't hate. The vast majority are boring and banal. If you're following your textbook to the letter each day, I guarantee you're putting your classes to sleep.

I'll tell you a story. As a first-year English teacher, I was handed a teacher's guide to accompany the literature book. I promptly stuffed it into a file cabinet and then forgot about it. (Hey, what can I say? I was busy.) Then one day in November, I stumbled across it and began to page through. I was stunned to find the literature questions as predictable as sleet in January—and about as much fun: "Why do you think Billy was angry at his mother? Possible answers: She was unwilling to let him grow up. She wanted to control his actions. She was afraid he would leave her."

I was stunned. Where were the meaty prompts about anger sometimes being passive-aggressive and how someone might learn to recognize it in another person and in oneself? Where was the discussion about the complex push-pull between parent and adolescent child? Where were the suggestions on how a teenager might make the transition period a bit easier on his mom or dad, and therefore on himself?

By sheer instinct I had already sparked some pretty animated discussions, which included the kids' bouncing personal experiences off each other, learning plenty from what others were going through, and (of course) forging closer relationships with peers by talking freely in class.

I know by now that you're probably clutching your heart in dismay, wondering on what planet any teacher would be permitted to disregard curricular demands. But this was 1968, remember, when there was little monitoring and even less assistance. New teachers were left totally on their own. Over the years, teachers' guides evolved and became much more demanding. But by then I'd long since learned to use them as springboards rather than road maps.

Want more creative lesson plans? Ask yourself each time you write one: Why should anyone find this interesting? What's in it for *her*? After a few months it becomes instinctive, and you won't even consider presenting material on poisonous spiders, quadratic equations, or John Keats without finding a way to make it cool and relevant. Think of that dull guide as a cake mix. Don't just add water and eggs, as it says on the back of the box. Try folding in some chocolate pudding, some raspberries, and a dash of cinnamon.

# Don't read newspapers before going to class.

They'll be filled with horror stories about irresponsible, vacant teenagers who toss bricks onto passing cars from overpasses and rob the elderly of their Social Security checks. Not to mention articles about teachers who sexually abuse their students. The media can never be counted on for a fair or realistic assessment of today's young people—or of their teachers, for that matter. The freaks are always the focus. You don't need this steady diet of negativity.

> "It is the mark of an educated mind to be able to entertain a thought without accepting it."
> **—ARISTOTLE**

# Get enough rest.

Yeah, sure. Hard to pull off when the alarm rings every day before dawn. And as I have said before, you never quite get used to it. You can, however, put an occasional remedy in place.

During the last five years of my career, when I was feeling pretty old and tired, I began habitually going to bed at 7:00 P.M. every Wednesday night, especially during the dark months, November through March. It really seemed to help.

> "Getting my lifelong weight struggle under control has come from a process of treating myself as well as I treat others in every way."
>
> **—OPRAH WINFREY**

# Extra duties are a fact of life.

They're considered part of the job of teaching school, and many times, sad to say, you won't be given a choice. Only after you've put in at least twenty years can you (sometimes) politely demure—or at least select your own poison.

Try not to get stuck with an extracurricular for which you are totally unsuited. The best pickings go to the earliest volunteers, so choose something you'll enjoy, like chess club, and speak up fast. Perhaps you'll snag something that pays. (Notice I didn't say "pays fairly." There is no such thing in public education.) An activity that is seasonal rather than year-round has its benefits too, but the stipend will be significantly less.

And then there are the daily assignments that everyone draws: study hall, achievement test proctoring, hall duty, cafeteria duty, and potty patrol. In elementary schools, add safety patrol, bus duty, recess duty . . . Teachers categorize all of these chores as demeaning, and they're absolutely right. That time would certainly be better spent grading tests. But face it—you're a handy source of cheap labor because you're already on the premises. The only thing that has changed in recent years is that administrators no longer consider themselves exempt, as they once did. They're in the cafeteria, standing right next to you.

Speaking of which, as a new teacher you may also be drafted for every planning committee under the sun, with topics ranging from revamping protocol for parental pickups to rewriting the entire curriculum. Don't even consider skipping a meeting; administrators are fierce about attendance. You won't be allowed to grade papers, either, without appearing insufferably rude.

Your only option is to put a good face on it, hope that your group's recommendations ultimately help the school run more smoothly—and watch how miffed the staff gets whenever decisions are made *without* their input. Committee meetings may be a nuisance, but the alternative can be far worse.

# It's the little things that will drive you nuts.

Like being unable to work in your own room during your unassigned period because someone else has a class in there. (For too many years my "office" was my car, even during the winter. One year I was granted a desk in the women's restroom, within easy earshot of constantly flushing toilets.)

Like spending forty precious minutes in line for the copier, only to have it jam on you ten seconds before the bell.

Like enduring announcements every three minutes that instruct certain homerooms to report to the gym for school pictures, and having four kids at a time get up and leave—yet being told that you should still conduct class as if it were a normal day.

I know, it all sounds like petty complaining—unless you're the one who has to deal with it. Seek solace in the fact that every teacher alive has walked in your shoes. Then take a deep breath and look directly into the face of the most delightful, well-behaved, eager-to-learn child in your class.

# Take an occasional mental health day.

If you're feeling lousy about life in general, or you just need a few moments of silence, or you just can't face the constant juggling act, call in ill. (It's true; you are.) Once, perhaps twice a year tops should do it. Continuing to kill yourself week after week doesn't do anyone any favors. And being continually grumpy with your students does far more damage than using up a day of sick leave.

> " Keeping your body healthy is an expression of gratitude to the whole cosmos—the trees, the clouds, everything. "
> —THICH NHAT HANH

# Be kind to subs.

This is one position that can truly be hell on Earth. Substitutes are sitting ducks for every wiseacre and disciplinary challenge within miles. The only exceptions are those fortunate enough to specialize in specific schools, so they get to know most of the kids. Otherwise, they feel like Old West deputy sheriffs who are assigned to keep order in lawless streets, yet aren't issued any handguns.

On the secondary level, you'll want to leave at least one day's lesson plan with instructions in your center desk drawer at all times. (You never know when a flu bug will suddenly hit you at 10:00 P.M.) Keep it simple: a brief reading and a Q-A worksheet. Very little work will take place anyway, as kids rarely take subs seriously, so reassure your replacement that he merely needs to hand out and later collect papers. Expecting him to be you, conducting business as usual, is, with all but the most exceptional college-bound groups, expecting too much.

In elementary grades, your task will be more time-consuming because you'll need to fill an entire day. You might consider a standard absence plan, such as a series of reviews of previously taught material in each subject, or group projects that fall under the heading of enrichment. Once again, the sub will fill a vital role, but he or she will not be you. Don't be surprised if when you return your kids greet you with more enthusiasm than usual. Kids crave normality much more than disruption or unpredictability.

# Know when it's time to leave.

Everyone has occasional bad days, but if you're waking up each morning dreading the prospect of facing another roomful of kids, then it's time to reevaluate. Some jobs can be muddled through with little or no enthusiasm. Teaching isn't one of them.

If your anger and resentment become overwhelming, the kids will sense it—and they'll begin to resent you. Even worse, you run the risk of doing untold psychological damage, because despite what they may claim, young people always think they're the cause. If, heaven forbid, you find yourself repeatedly crushing a child's spirit with too-harsh reprimands or long-winded tirades, you should do everyone, including yourself, a favor. Get out.

Or it may be that you need only a pep talk from a dedicated veteran. That person can speak from personal experience about the days, weeks, or months during which he or she felt mired in a sense of futility—yet somehow found a way to climb out of it and feel a renewed energy and optimism. (Need I add that these folks have earned their rightful places in heaven?)

I once talked to a new teacher who by early December had already decided she'd made a dreadful mistake and was planning to turn in her resignation at the semester's end. There was nothing she enjoyed about the profession or her students, she said, and besides, it was too doggone much work. I felt saddened for her. But then I remembered how many other people I'd met over the years who admitted they'd lasted only a year or two in the classroom.

Not everyone is suited to be a teacher. There's no shame in that. The better part of wisdom is knowing yourself.

# Pardon the interruptions.

Constant PA announcements and passes from the office are additional unpleasant facts of life. You have no choice but to grin and bear them. This will never get easy, particularly if you've constructed a lesson that calls for setting a sentimental mood—like the death scene in *Romeo and Juliet.*

At the worst possible moment, just when everyone's feeling romantic and tragic, and you're about to pass around the box of tissues, you'll hear that jarring bleat of the speaker and a much-too-loud command for John Jones to please move his car out of the circle. (I've never understood the need to interrupt the concentration of two thousand people to address the personal transgression of just one.)

Eventually you'll develop a trick or two for dealing with it . . . such as deliberately stopping like a statue in midsentence with your mouth open and one finger raised until the announcement is over, or insisting that passes from office monitors lie unacknowledged on your desk until the main part of your lesson is completed. But the not-so-subtle message is obvious: the box—or perhaps I should say the speaker behind it—feels that he is more important than you are. In a literal sense he is right. In a cosmic sense, we all know better. Which could be why these folks keep on interrupting.

One thing that I found incredibly empowering in later years was when my class would groan at the disruption right along with me. That simple act spoke volumes. My irritation vanished. As a united front, we had become impervious to all invaders.

Whenever I visualize public education as it should be (a pipe dream, to be sure), I always include a study hall or homework period, even in elementary grades, from which students can be pulled out at will by counselors and nurses, so that class time would always proceed uninterrupted.

# Beware the killer schedule.

Sooner or later, you'll probably get one. And it can be awful.

For example, I know several teachers who've been assigned six preps. That means a different subject or grade level every period, which means that each night, all year long, they are writing six separate lesson plans. Elementary teachers who have split classes (for example, second and third grade in one room) also get to do two jobs for the price of one. How lucky can you get?

And then there's "traveling." That means your school doesn't have enough classrooms for everyone, and a few unfortunate souls must move from room to room every period while the regular tenants are on duty somewhere else—like study hall. You get to push a rolling cart with handouts, textbooks, and supplies piled high and therefore vulnerable to careening traffic. (Keep your eyes open and your arms wrapped firmly around your vehicle.)

But that's not even the worst-case scenario. One teacher I know traveled between two different buildings. She had a fourth-period class in one and a fifth-period class in the other—a mile across town.

Okay, I'm starting to sound a little frustrated here. That's because I too was a traveler for sixteen of my thirty-one years. Those assignments weren't anything personal; they were merely due to my taking two separate maternity leaves and moving from junior high to high school teaching—thereby forfeiting all of my seniority each time. Yes, it can happen that easily.

But "challenging" doesn't even begin to describe what it was like to be constantly on the move. I saw one new teacher break down in tears over it. She'd just been reprimanded by an administrator for being late to a class!

There are some remedies for this educational idiocy. First, remember that you can't possibly violate the laws of physics and be two people, let alone in two places at once. Second, marshal the understanding of your students. Explain to them that if you seem highly stressed, it isn't their fault; you may just need to pause in the hallway for a deep breath before beginning a lesson. Third, demand at least one desk drawer in each room so that you can stow a few things and feel a bit less like a human U-Haul. If you're an elementary teacher, you'll quickly learn to encourage small study and work groups, with you "floating" from place to place.

Fourth, don't let anyone try to convince you that this kind of handicap is no big deal. It is.

Finally, pray for a better situation next year.

# Do most of your preparation well in advance.

That means writing tests, worksheets, outlines of units, and lesson plans during the summer. Otherwise you will often be working well past 11:00 P.M. throughout the entire school year. It's a short road to an early demise.

> "Before everything else, getting ready is the secret to success.
> **—HENRY FORD**

> "To be prepared is half the victory.
> **—MIGUEL DE CERVANTES**

# Stay an extra hour after school several days each week rather than taking loads of paperwork home.

You'll get far more done without the phone ringing, the dog barking, or the spaghetti boiling over. Besides, some nights, given family crises and reruns of *Seinfeld*, much of what gets lugged home will never make it out of your trunk.

> " The time to repair the roof is when the sun is shining. "
> —**JOHN F. KENNEDY**

# Entertainment is not a dirty word.

Everyone knows that lecturing is the least effective way of getting points across. So why do we still do it? What's wrong with sparking your lessons with costumes, props, film clips, and unexpected visits from appropriate guests? Easy. It takes extra time, energy, planning, and often money. But the results are worth it.

Once, during a discussion of Sigmund Freud's talking cure, otherwise known as psychoanalysis, I told my class that people often find their own solutions after talking out their problems, and that a good therapist just knows how to ask the right questions. They were incredulous. So I invited a psychiatric social worker to demonstrate the questioning technique with two student volunteers. The insights they gained in those brief twenty-minute sessions, they told me later, were astonishing.

Okay, I can see you shrugging. What sort of wisdom can be gained in twenty minutes? First, the students became aware that delving deeper into their own psyches uncovered truths they didn't know were there. Second, they had to admit that some professionals really did know what they were doing.

Just be careful; there's a fine line between enrichment and wasting time. Running an entire John Wayne movie during a lesson on the American frontier is wasteful. Running a filmed version of *Macbeth* after you've read the play, however, is enrichment.

In general, you shouldn't rush to cover every last shred of designated material. Better to take your time and let things sink in. Periodically rewind and briefly review what's already been covered.

Always remember to ask yourself: What are my students really supposed to learn here? It will keep you pretty much on track—because if you can't supply an answer with real substance, it's time to go back and start over.

# You'll meet only about nine different kids in your entire career.

After about five years or so, you'll start to recognize parallel behavior patterns and similar character traits. Every class seems to have a rebel, a brain, a delinquent, a bully, a recluse, a queen bee, a misunderstood genius, a clown, and (in high school) a teenage parent. Give yourself enough time, and you'll get so good at spotting types that when they talk about their problems, you'll be able to predict what will happen next. Because you're wise, experienced, observant, and a grown-up, you'll often be right—which will thoroughly spook the kids. They'll claim you're psychic. Let them think that.

This awareness of types can also come in handy when you need to write comments on report cards. Store them on your computer for easy retrieval when you realize that Everett strongly reminds you of Lester from three years earlier. Are they unique individuals in their own right? Of course. But you may have used perfect word choices to describe Lester's special talent. Perhaps they'll work for Everett too, thereby sparing you fifteen minutes of mental groping.

# Everything you've heard about students' emotional baggage is true.

I received a jarring lesson pretty early, during my second year of teaching. It came in the person of a seventh-grade girl. Ellen did everything slowly. She moved slowly, completed her class work slowly, and her homework not at all. She annoyed me. So one day I kept her after class and presented a stern, teachery lecture on listening to directions and getting her assignments in on time.

Only after I finally wound down did Ellen admit haltingly that her mother was seriously ill, and she was spending all her time at home preparing meals, spoon-feeding, and reading aloud. This twelve-year-old was single-handedly assuming a duty that would throw any adult's life into a maelstrom.

Of course I felt lousy. But now, over three decades later, I have to thank Ellen. In my incredible arrogance I'd made a child's shabby little life even shabbier. I resolved never to do it again. From then on, I asked lots of questions before launching into anything resembling a hard-nosed speech.

# Large classes aren't the bogeymen you've been led to believe.

Teachers seem totally fixated on class sizes under twenty-five. It's even a bone of contention during contract negotiations. Ask any teacher what would make the biggest improvement in his quality of instruction, and the answer will nearly always be smaller classes.

Granted, large numbers dictate increased paperwork. And as an English teacher, I carried home busloads of it. But I think we may be overlooking the enormous benefits of playing to a full house.

And because I counted so many administrators and guidance counselors as friends, I could sympathize with their plight. What were they supposed to do with three hundred students enrolled at each grade level and only nine English teachers?

At one point I was teaching a large class of at-risk seniors, all eager to graduate on time and get on with their lives—and therefore humbly grateful that I was willing to take them in, so that they wouldn't need to attend summer school. Guess what? Discipline problems evaporated. Class discussions became more animated. Camaraderie increased.

As strange as it sounds, I soon grew to prefer larger groups. Small ones actually seemed cliquish and reticent by comparison. And there was something very empowering about seeing my kids race to class so that they could get a good seat, rather than hanging out in the hall and then being relegated to sitting on the radiator. When they looked around in amazement at my high numbers, they instantly stopped wondering about my commitment—which in turn stopped cold all discontented muttering. In the long run, it made classroom control easier, not harder.

Am I advocating, then, your tacit acceptance of forty students in each class? No, of course not. Ideally, that should never happen. Just don't panic when your enrollment hits thirty-five. It's really not the end of the world. It may, in fact, be a great start.

Of course I need to add that this philosophy applies only to secondary classes. Virtually everyone who knows anything about how children learn insists that class sizes must be under twenty in grades K–3 for optimal learning to take place. Most of us would extend that recommendation through sixth grade.

# Beware of germs.

During the winter of 1968–1969 (my first year of teaching), I had six colds, one right after another. Obviously, I was catching every virus floating around. Then one afternoon I spotted one of my students sneezing, using his vocabulary quiz as a shield, and then handing in the paper. To me.

That day changed my life. I took action. A box of tissues became a permanent fixture on my desk, and I didn't care how much money I spent on replacements during the frigid months when each box seemed to empty within hours.

If you're lucky enough to have your own classroom, keep a steady supply of disinfectant spray and a roll of paper towels in your closet. Swab down your desk and computer keyboard—daily. While you're at it, clean off your students' desks every week or so too.

Digging in your heels and claiming this isn't your job will lead to physical ruination. The average teacher's desk, studies claim, carries four hundred times more contagious bacteria than a public toilet seat. Think about it.

# Today's kids are so independent that we should probably coin a new word.

In some ways this is a good thing. They're less gullible than we were; they constantly question authority.

At the same time, too many are fixated on easy money, instant fame, and finding shortcuts. That independence that dictates their driving their own (new) cars, whipping out their own credit cards, buying fast food and video games, and attending school only when they feel like it is temporary. Eventually they'll learn that all goodies are bought and paid for with their own sweat. So as teachers we should be encouraging a free will that is less cloaked in consumerism. Whatever's new and nifty will eventually wear out or fade from public view. An interest-bearing savings account, in contrast, only grows better with time.

# Be alert for happy accidents and blessings in disguise.

It was fall, 1969. German textbooks had been ordered in June, but by late August they still hadn't arrived. I was in a total quandary. How was I supposed to teach a first-year foreign language class of ninth graders without any grammar books?

"Do the best you can," my principal told me. "They'll be here shortly."

Nine weeks later, they still hadn't shown. But by then the class and I had embarked on a totally conversational approach, engaging in a daily question-and-answer dialogue (basic models were on the board) consisting of references to current events, inside jokes, and good-natured ribbing. Everyone scrambled to purchase English-German dictionaries to come up with their own new vocabulary words. Fellow teachers tapped on my door, asking me to please keep the laughter down; they could hear it three rooms away.

One day in late November, I entered my classroom and saw thirty brand-new books piled high on my desk. I shrugged at the sight of them. Throughout the rest of the year we used them for short grammar lessons, readings, and written work, but then quickly returned to our usual irreverent class discussions—in German.

At a class reunion thirty-five years later, a large group of graying fifty-year-olds hung out in a circle, trading jokes and mild insults—in German.

I just stood there and beamed.

# Understand the politics of study hall.

If you ever doubt that you have a rare talent, then try to imagine anyone else entering a cafeteria full of two hundred rowdy teenagers on the first day of school and within fifteen minutes having everyone quiet, settled in their assigned seats, and working . . . well, okay, quiet. Most schools will (thank goodness) assign two or three teachers for the really heavy loads (usually near the end of the school day), so you can divide your enrollments by the total number of supervisors. Generally this is done alphabetically—but don't expect things to stay that neat as the year progresses. Schedule changes will continue even through final exam week; kids despise study halls and will do almost anything to get out of them.

What used to be study time two generations ago has turned into a mere zone-out time. Study hall still exists only because it's the best way to warehouse students not scheduled for class during the state's required number of attendance hours.

So you should do yourself several favors. First, seat everyone with empty chairs between them. Second, seat everyone facing the back wall, so that enterers and leavers aren't subjected to scrutinizing and catcalls. Third, use study hall to your advantage, holding one-on-one conferences with students who need to catch up on back assignments or who just need to talk about their lives.

Otherwise, strongly consider letting the kids doze. (Many schools allow this now, so this is one battle you don't need to fight alone.) Most students are sleep deprived, after all, and your insisting that everyone be actively productive with a textbook open just seems to borrow trouble.

You, however, must somehow manage to stay awake.

# These are lifetime relationships.

We all know we're not supposed to play favorites, but . . .

There will always be some kids to whom you relate better than others. And there will be a few who, regardless of whether you teach first grade or twelfth, spark a flash of instant, soul-mate-level recognition.

There will also be a few who, despite your best efforts, are as troublesome and difficult to reach as a burr under a saddle. (They may be soul mates too, but in a much different sense.)

You'll want to keep your distance a bit while your shining stars are in your class, so that they won't be embarrassed by your effusive attention and the others won't feel overlooked—but once the year is over, don't be surprised if you hear from those special ones. And hear from them. And hear from them.

You'll likely be attending their college graduations, their weddings, their baby showers, their parents' funerals . . . No, I'm not kidding.

Some teachers may frown at the thought of violating their personal boundaries. Where does this job end? Well, that's a very individual choice. My own decision was not to erect any barriers. To this day, if a former student wants to stay in touch, I'm delighted.

There's something touchingly eternal about reuniting five, ten, or twenty years later and hearing about children and grandchildren, marriages and divorces, all of life's triumphs and adversities. You get to see twelve-year-old faces superimposed over those of forty-year-olds. You get to hear numerous accolades and heartfelt thanks. You get to smile at even former irritants who will cry and hug you.

Every year on my birthday I get five phone calls from former students: one from my first year of teaching, one from my fifth, one from my twelfth, one from my nineteenth, and one from my twenty-ninth. Every year I feel honored to be so fondly remembered by such a scattered group. It often feels as if they've come to represent nearly three generations of teaching memories.

There are a few bizarre offshoots of this soul-mate thing. Once in a while you'll get lucky, meet a student's parents, and feel just as close to them as to their child. You'll be asked to dinner, know the security of kind and loving solace for your parent-teacher concerns. (In the long run it makes up for some of the unpleasant characters you may eventually meet.)

And finally, you'll encounter one or two who feel it's their mission to make your life a horror show and will constantly go out of their way to let you know how much they dislike you. Don't take it personally. Anyone who pours that much energy into a bad relationship has some underlying issues that have little to do with you.

> **I've learned that people will forget what you said, people will forget what you did, but people will never forget how you made them feel.**
> **—MAYA ANGELOU**

You may even find, as I did several times, that a student masks his or her attraction to you with baiting and harassment. I once ran into a girl five years after graduation and was greeted with a hug. When I laughingly recalled how she'd tried to sabotage every one of my class discussions, she shook her head ruefully. "I really admired you," she said. "But back then I couldn't admit it, not even to myself. You seemed so smart and so perfect, I knew I could never measure up."

We still occasionally meet for lunch.

Another odd thing began to happen after I'd been a teacher for about fifteen years: a former student would suddenly pop into my mind after months or even years. Within twenty-four hours, there he'd be, standing at my door, grinning, saying, "I have no idea why, but I woke up today and knew I had to come and see you. I even took a day off work!"

All of this merely reinforces what a divine calling this teaching business really is. That line about a teacher affecting eternity covers only half the reality. The truth is, our students remain in our hearts just as much and for just as long.

# You won't reach everyone—but you'll be pleasantly surprised at your success rate.

If your attitude is positive and you generally enjoy teaching, it's hard to go wrong, and by the end of the year you'll know it. Save room on your final exam to ask for input: "Is there anything you think I should change?" You'll get your share of "Stop wearing those lame neckties," but you'll also receive a host of warm compliments. Kids who you'd always assumed didn't give a rat's behind will tell you how much they enjoyed your class.

Save these testimonials. They'll carry you through your rougher times. At the end of your career, you'll have accumulated trunks full.

> " Scores are too literal; scores do not represent the union of the intellectual and emotional. Scores have no soul. "
> **—JOAN CUTULY**

# 6

# Rules and
# Routines

*We are all responsible
for the choices we make.
[Students] should be
taught that it is their
job to figure out the best
choices.*

—**William Glasser**

# Ask for help sooner rather than later.

Start with your department chairperson; that's what he or she is there for. Or your mentor teacher, if your district has such a program. If you're feeling overwhelmed or discouraged, say so. We can all remember what our first few years were like and how inadequate we felt. Most of us veterans also have files and files of extra materials that we can easily spare. Some of us are even willing to take on a disciplinary hard case who has you fuming. So ask. And just think: someday, two decades from now, you'll get to pay it forward!

# Bring your principal a solution rather than a problem.

I was once assigned three German classes in one. That's right: first-, second-, and third-year students, all in one room, all during one period. I felt like one of those circus performers who kept trying to spin ten plates at once.

Finally, after two weeks, I told my principal that it just wasn't working, and I suggested scheduling the first-year group on Mondays and Wednesdays, the second and third on Tuesdays and Thursdays, and everybody together on Fridays. (That way, study hall rosters wouldn't increase too dramatically.) To my surprise, he went for it, and the rest of the year ran relatively smoothly.

The next time you're facing what appears to be an insurmountable obstacle, before you approach your principal, be sure to come armed with a solution. Offer it quickly. Present not just a dilemma but also a resolution. Even if she ultimately suggests something different, you won't be perceived as just dumping a problem in her lap.

# Stop your class two minutes early.

It took me twenty-five years to figure this one out, but eventually I learned to build in a time buffer. Two minutes is usually enough. Some teachers use the final moments (if not interrupted by the PA) to ask if anyone has any comments. I usually wound up with students milling around my desk, still asking questions or just being friendly.

The naysayers who liked to remind me of how much time I was wasting every year were ignoring two things. First, nobody was listening in those final moments anyway. Second, my mental health was probably better than theirs, because rather than continually losing my concluding point, I got to summarize my lessons in my own way. Two minutes per period each day may well have saved me two years in anger management therapy.

For the elementary level, you can adapt this idea with periodic stand-and-yawn-and-stretch breaks (something you're probably already doing). A prearranged signal, such as flicking the lights or blowing a bicycle horn, can alert everyone that it's time to get back to business.

There are no breaks during a teacher's day. You must save your life by creating your own.

# Forget bathroom breaks.

You can write passes for your students who have restroom emergencies—but sad to say, you can't write one for yourself. And you can't just go whenever you feel the urge. Schools forbid teachers to leave their classrooms for any reason—unless you manage to flag down a hall monitor to stand at your door and supervise while you're gone.

This wreaks total havoc if you've eaten something spicy, if you're female, or if you've simply had too much coffee that morning. And if you're in the habit of carrying around a water bottle, you'll definitely need to rethink that.

Go between classes? Nope. Teachers are required to stand at their doors and monitor hallway traffic. Face it. If you have five straight classes, you will be in bladder hell every single day. The only solution is an arrangement with the teacher next door to have him dart back and forth between both rooms for five minutes. Otherwise . . . you have no choice but to hold it.

It always seemed ironic to me that in a profession where we're constantly expected to cater to the needs of dozens of others, we aren't permitted to have any of our own, not even the most basic physical ones. After three decades of repeated urinary infections, once I retired from teaching, I never had another one.

There might be a connection.

# Rethink seating charts.

There's something disconcerting about six rows of six seats apiece, all lined up to face a single teacher's desk. It makes classroom camaraderie a struggle. Half the kids can't even see each other, let alone hear what anyone else has to say.

So I designed my own floor plan: an empty landing strip dead center. Five rows of three seats apiece on each side, facing each other. Advantages: nobody sits in a "rear" row. There are plenty of friends—front, back, and sideways—to converse with. Wait! Do you want that? In the best of all worlds, yes!

Part of great classroom management is having a group that gets along well enough to enjoy rousing debates and discussions. Also, if the teacher is always a mere five feet away, it's tougher to form pockety little cliques.

You may not like this particular option, so get out a piece of graph paper and try designing your own. I'll just add that whenever a new class walked in on the first day and spotted this strange arrangement, they were instantly charmed: "This is different. What's going on?"

Also, I occasionally tried that seminar-like, full-circle layout too, but none of my classes ever embraced it. I finally figured out that they felt closer when they faced a landing strip!

# Rethink homework.

This one is as controversial as it gets. One side says, "All kids need homework; it reinforces daily lessons and teaches that not all work takes place while on the clock." The other side says, "Homework levels have become intolerable. No child should be working on assignments at the kitchen table far into the night." Both viewpoints are absolutely correct.

My stance? Homework reinforces nothing if it doesn't get done. And except for those committed college-bound and advanced-placement groups, it generally doesn't. The world has changed. Children have soccer practice and ballet lessons. Teenagers have after-school jobs. Families want to run out for pizza. Few parents will sit down and quiz their kids on spelling words at 9:00 P.M. Everyone's exhausted.

So I think teachers need to build in more class time to get the work done. Won't this take away from your lecturing? Yes. Is that a bad thing? Perhaps not. It forces you to say more by saying less.

We also need to rethink quantities. Do you really need to assign sixty-six nightly math problems? Wouldn't sixteen every other night do just as well?

Because this is such a thorny issue right now, I think you have the right to make your own decision regarding what works best for both you and your students. Whatever you choose to do, you'll find plenty of data to back you up.

# Rethink raising hands.

More blasphemy! Tar and feather this woman!

No, give me a moment here to relate my own experience. In many cases, when an enthusiastic discussion was under way, hand raising became unnecessary. It just slowed things down. Everybody was willing to give everyone else his or her share of time. And when things got too loud, I quieted everyone and then gave the floor back not to myself, but to whomever had just been shouted over. Strangely enough, this approach worked. But only after my commanding presence and strong voice were firmly in place. Hey, not all noise is bad. And not all sudden light-bulb insights should come from the teacher.

# There are times when you can no longer be sweet, helpful, or complacent.

Like when you encounter physical threats, lying, bullying, cruelty, or fraud.

Like when a student mutters under his breath, "You'd better be careful walking out to your car tonight. You never can tell what will happen." Like when a student is clearly tormenting someone else with comments or "accidental" bumps in the hallway. Like when you spot a girl handing back a boy's ring, and he spits in her face. Like when you catch a student in the act of stealing another classmate's work and then writing his own name on it.

That's when you call in the big gun, the student's administrator.

I'll risk sounding paranoid, but I must add this: if there's a classroom incident, get to the administrator before the student does. Otherwise, his or her attitude may be colored by a whole laundry list of transgressions and unfair acts that you've supposedly committed. And then you're really screwed—because then it becomes a sad matter of the student's word against yours, and you could very well lose.

The remedy for this is . . .

# Document every altercation; keep a daily log.

This will feel like a second job, but you absolutely must do it. Every time Jessie falls asleep in class, mouths off, or acts like a general pain, you'll need to write it down. Dates, times, details. What she wore, what you wore. I'm kidding, but not totally. This isn't the school administrators' fault. Today, with a lawyer on every block, parents are too ready to take every detention to court. If you pull out a written history dating back several months, you'll be much harder to beat into submission.

Don't trust your memory. It's already filled with enough trivia. Put everything in writing.

# Make friends with Lowe's and the Home Depot.

After many years of spending valuable moments at the beginning of each period catching up the previous day's absentees, I finally lined up six plastic milk crates (you can find them for $5 or less at one of these two big-box stores, generally cheaper than anywhere else) near the window (a different color for each class period) and posted the week's assignments, along with proper handouts in each. Whether someone had been gone one day or five, she could bring herself up to speed in record time with no further assistance from me. Whenever someone approached and asked, "What did I miss?" I'd just smile and point. Eventually, like by around April, they caught on and stopped asking.

I also placed another crate on my desk for assignments to be handed in as the kids entered or left. Those milk crates must have easily saved me thirty minutes of aggravation every week. You do the math.

# Store all papers.

Perhaps you'll be lucky enough to have a five-drawer file cabinet and an office willing to hand over 160 manila folders. If not, you'll be buying those folders (and more milk crates!) yourself. Do it. It's worth it.

Use a different colored crate for each class. Because filing papers into each kid's folder will rob you of half your life, hire an eager, reliable student to do it during his or her study hall instead. You conduct class, while little Ralph or Doris does your grunt work. Buy him or her fast-food gift certificates to compensate.

You'll notice I'm not suggesting that students file their own papers. There's a good reason for this. Opportunities for theft, loss, or plagiarism are huge. Also, every so often, a kid who's done no work will claim that he did, and that you simply "lost" it. His parents will back him. The burden of proof will be on you, and that proof will be easier if there haven't been multiple hands rifling through your stuff.

Also, keep those papers behind lock and key. Trust me on this one. A fraud attempt may occur only once every five years, but if you haven't taken precautions, you'll want to hang yourself with your own scarf.

# Don't get too bent out of shape about dress and grooming.

Back in the day (1970, to be exact), administrators everywhere had their panties in a wad when students were insisting on the right to wear jeans to school. Oh, the world was coming to an end. We already had peace signs, love beads, and long, unwashed hair. Now jeans.

New teachers like me were saying things like, "I don't care if the kids come to school naked, as long as they show up." Oh, little did we know. Three decades later I was dealing with bare midriffs, visible navels, cleavage, butt cracks—and pink hair.

But you may be surprised to hear that I still feel to a large extent the same way I did forty years ago. "Dressing out" is a fairly harmless (and very temporary) form of teenage rebellion. No twenty-four-year-old CPA will likely show up on his first day of work with pink hair. And he'll wear a long-sleeved shirt to cover his tattoos.

Here's what I told my students: "It is every younger generation's duty to shock and outrage their elders. The easiest way to do that is through clothing, hair, jewelry, and body art. And you, my dears, have done an *outstanding* job on that account! For which you deserve a hearty round of applause." Clap, clap, clap. They loved it.

But I always had to laugh whenever a kid proclaimed himself a rebel for wearing twelve face studs and a nose ring. I'd respond by saying, "You aren't a rebel. You look exactly like the rest of your age group. If you really want to rebel, try coming to school wearing a powder-pink leisure suit."

It went right over the kid's head ("What's a leisure suit?")—but I cracked myself up.

That said, we still need dress codes. We cannot tolerate the exposure of certain body parts, or lewd sayings on T-shirts. But we should also take comfort in the fact that today's children will be tomorrow's parents. And then *we* get to sit back and watch the fun.

You as a teacher are well within your rights to require a student to turn an objectionable garment inside out—or maybe even report to the office. Just don't let it ruin your whole day.

And remember, he will eventually have a fourteen-year-old daughter. Clap, clap, clap.

# Call parents regularly.

Most teachers feel that lifelong relationships with students are the real rewards of teaching, and they're right. But there's another equally delightful perk—friendships with parents. Great parents can see and comment on your exceptional talent and dedication far sooner than their kids do—sometimes before you're even aware of them yourself. And every one, without exception, is touched and grateful that an unrelated adult has taken an avid interest in his or her child's progress and learning.

Will you need to make the first approach and perhaps carry the burden of keeping those phone calls coming? Probably. But this is one investment that's worth every extra minute. The moment little Ronnie or Susie gets lazy or causes trouble, you'll have a very determined ally in getting him or her back on track.

Don't wait for conference nights. Turnouts are always disappointingly low. You'll feel so lonely, in fact, that you'll be tempted to greet the three parents who do show up with tearful hugs. I once heard about a school district that required that all report cards be picked up by parents. Every quarter. In person. Not a bad idea.

# Never pass up an opportunity to convey a compliment to a colleague.

If one of your students mentions in passing that Mr. Chambers is the best history teacher he's ever had, you need to make it your mission to let Mr. Chambers know. Consider this, in fact, nothing less than a duty. Chances are he'll never hear it from the kid in question, and I guarantee you'll make your friend's week. Maybe even his year.

Your student, by the way, should be told how much it means to teachers to receive such compliments.

> " We make a living by what we get, we make a life by what we give. "
> —**WINSTON CHURCHILL**

# Be careful what you say in class; someone may still be repeating it fifty years later.

It's a rare teacher who can keep his or her personal politics out of the classroom. Practice prefacing most of your soapbox tirades, therefore, with "This is only my opinion, but . . ."

Also, there will be days when you think you're saying some very wise things, but no one seems to be listening. Then there will be days when you toss off some random remark, and twenty years down the line, a former student visits and tells you that your statement changed his entire life. And that he plans to repeat it to his grandchildren.

# 7

# Keeping It Creative

"*No one can teach a subject in the same way two years running. The alternatives are to let your teaching petrify by neglect or constantly to refresh it by transfusions of new vitality and interest.*"

—**Gilbert Highet**

# Ask yourself regularly: Can I do better?

Of course you can. You don't want to continue using the same old, yellowed notes and one-dimensional plans year after year—because everything you do should be tied into what's going on in the world this month, not last. Society is ever evolving, and there's always plenty of material out there. A great perk: having an inquiring mind tickles not only your students' interest but also your own.

Each summer, you should go through your lesson files with the intention of pruning. Keep whatever wowed 'em. Update or discard whatever didn't.

Of course the current standardization movement has made the creativity you seek far more elusive. But the intention was never for everyone to march in lockstep. You should still tuck freshness inside regimentation. In a moment I'll offer specifics on how to do that.

# Be alert to any and all possibilities: How can I use this in class?

You'll find ideas in newspaper and magazine articles, on PBS specials, in people you meet at parties. Soon the whole world becomes your lesson plan. It's like carrying a camera. You see more, so you photograph more. You photograph more, so you see more.

Consider instituting a "What did you learn this week?" segment, where you begin by talking about what you heard Dr. Oz say on *Oprah* about flesh-eating bacteria or about brain stimulation to eliminate food cravings. Then take volunteers from the class to join in or offer their own examples.

# Cultivate a genuine passion for your subject matter.

And convey it. Even if your students can't always share your excitement about quadratic equations or the Civil War, at least they can see why you feel the magic. Don't be afraid to sound a tad foolish. There may a budding mathematician or a Bull Run reenacter sitting in the last row. And the guy who weeps with joy at the sight of a well-oiled motor will be able to relate to your affection for, say, alligators.

> Only passions, great passions, can elevate the soul to great things.
> —**DENIS DIDEROT**

# Remember your three roles.

First, intrigue. Second, share knowledge. Third, ask thoughtful, open-ended questions. Remember, great lessons aren't about dispensing dry facts or even showing students the "errors" in their thinking. They're about entertaining alternate possibilities.

Perhaps genetics have more to do with contracting diseases than we realize. Perhaps honeybees are more critical to our food chain than biologists have presumed. Perhaps we should usher in the "fair tax" concept, which taxes all purchases at 25 percent and eliminates all other means for the government to pick our pockets.

> "The aim of education should be to teach us rather how to think, than what to think—rather to improve our minds, so as to enable us to think for ourselves, than to load the memory with thoughts of other men."
>
> **—BILL BEATTIE**

What's far more compelling, for example, than Lincoln's signing the Emancipation Proclamation in 1863 is his painful awareness that the path to civil rights would be neither straightforward nor easy. What's far more compelling than his enduring greatness is his constant depression and his feeling of failure. Look beyond the obvious. What can this teach us?

# Take advantage of youthful self-absorption.

Because kids already think everything is about them, make your lessons about them too. If, for instance, you're reading *The Scarlet Letter*, why not encourage your students to research how different societies have dealt with out-of-wedlock pregnancy. In seventeenth-century New England, Hester Prynne was forced to stand on a scaffold and endure public ridicule for three hours, then wear a scarlet A (for adulteress) on her bodice for the rest of her life. Some Middle Eastern countries still stone such women to death. What should we be doing in our own time to be less about punishments and more about discouraging our youth in regard to risky behavior? Also, what examples can we find these days of people saying they believe one thing but acting as if they believe another? Hester's hypocritical village snubbed her—but also took full advantage of her talent as a seamstress by paying her next to nothing for her hard work!

# Never teach a subject in isolation.

You'd better be all over the map. Tie in the artistry in math, the sociology in history, the psychology in literature. Shakespeare's plays are all wonderful studies of human behavior. Think about how Lady Macbeth manages to convince her husband to murder the king; she attacks his manhood. And later she drowns in guilt and remorse right along with him.

# Keep running lists of Eternal Human Truths, Eternal Human Dilemmas, Eternal Crimes Against Humanity *(regardless of your subject matter)*.

This will keep students from feeling as if their own futures are hopeless. Recall the Great Depression, the Holocaust, the London Blitz. (What was it you were saying about outrageous gas prices?)

Use poster board and add new examples throughout the school year. Yes, it can get scrawled and messy—just like life.

Here's an example to get you started. Add or subtract data as you wish:

## Eternal Human Truths.
There will always be a segment of any population, whether it's in a classroom or a nation, that will take the greatest advantage of the smallest privilege. That's why true freedom will always be elusive.

Schools cost far less than prisons, but we still don't get it. People who feel smart, capable, and successful don't rob the elderly or burn down neighbors' garages. We need to figure out how to start from the ground up, at birth, to eliminate all vestiges of diminishing others, and hence all attempts to make others feel diminished.

No group in history has ever given up its power willingly. The oppressed have always needed to "get ugly" before anything has changed. (Think civil rights, gay rights, the women's movement, and all revolutions for independence, including our own.) Ugly doesn't necessarily mean violent, but that's typically how things wind up—Gandhi and Dr. Martin Luther King Jr. being our most notable exceptions.

Of course these topics are most relevant in a history or government class. If you want to focus on science, do some research on Ignaz Semmelweiss, a Hungarian doctor in the 1840s. He recommended that postoperative surgeons wash their hands before examining birthing women. The doctors refused. Thousands of new mothers continued to die tragically from an infection known as childbed fever for many more decades due to their stubbornness.

If you simplify a bit, you can use these same examples for elementary grades too. Don't be surprised if one of your kids suggests adding something that sounds transparent at first, but later, through multiple discussions, takes on a more complex meaning. For example: it's really hard to be good all of the time. All kids know this—but it will be fun for them to explore exactly why.

# Remember to show the better side of human nature too.

That should be another ongoing list: Eternal Heroic Behavior. Begin with the New York firefighters on 9/11. Work both backward and forward. Let your students be on an active lookout for heroes, people who put others' welfare ahead of their own, even if it costs them their lives. Think of the men who put the women and children into the *Titanic*'s few lifeboats and then stood on deck, watching them drift away, knowing they were the ones going down with the ship.

It's also essential to point out that these people were by no means perfect. Consider Oskar Schindler, who was a member of the Nazi Party and began his divine mission with the sole purpose of making a fortune. Consider Princess Diana, whose goodwill inspired millions, yet she was most definitely, like all of us, a flawed person.

# Dramatize.

Act out Marc Antony's speech following Julius Caesar's death, or Hester Prynne's sentence. Costumes and props help. A bedsheet makes a fine toga. A doll from your little sister's toy box can be held in your arms against an embroidered scarlet A. Afraid the kids will make fun? So what? I found that even seniors looked forward to the days when I'd introduce new reading material as vividly as any attorney making opening remarks to a jury.

Let the kids do some similar dramatizing. Put some of history's villains on trial. (Charles Manson still insists he never committed a single violent act; he only convinced others to do so on his behalf.) Debate city concerns, such as curfews for teens. One fifth-grade teacher I knew would successfully assign stage productions of short scenes from Shakespeare—not acts, and certainly not entire plays, just scenes. Downsizing can be extremely effective.

## Dramatize even more, in ways that pull out all the stops.
Walk around the room on your hands while reciting multiplication tables. Stand atop your desk wearing a top hat to reenact the Gettysburg Address. Do your best Tom Cruise impersonation when playing the part of Romeo ("But soft . . ."). If you have a couch, then you should definitely jump on it.

Sing the French national anthem when talking about Paris. Make up rhymes and jingles for anything needing memorization. Insist that the class join you in finger-snapping rhythm when repeating math or spelling rules. Accumulate a variety of hats or witty message buttons; wear a different one each day.

# Move heaven and Earth to get access to a VCR or DVD player.

Films are as worthy as any other form of literature. Fourth graders who claim that they can't wait to grow up so that they can do whatever they want might enjoy a scene or two from *Freaky Friday*, which dispels the notion that being an adult offers unlimited freedom.

Talking about slavery? Run that scene from *Roots* where Kunta Kinte is entrapped in steel chains, doesn't quite understand what they are, and can only roar in desperate agony. Introducing *Hamlet*? Offer additional examples of teenage boys in crisis with well-chosen scenes, such as James Dean in *Rebel Without a Cause* and Judd Nelson in *The Breakfast Club*.

*Note:* When I say "scene," I mean just that. A thirty-second clip is usually sufficient to make your point. And don't forget to fill out the proper forms beforehand. It's one sheet at a time, filed with your administrator, so he or she knows what's going on. A headache—but it sure beats having an irate parent standing at your door the next morning.

One day, following my *Hamlet* introduction, a young man stopped after class. "I think I finally get it!" he declared. "It's just like you've been saying—all of those people in the past are still living inside us! We're all the same!"

I felt like celebrating.

# Intersperse specific student names when teaching a lesson that could otherwise descend into dullness.

"And, Hayley, wouldn't you love to know how the days of the week got their names?" Be sure to spread the love, so that no one feels excessively singled out. And keep smiling, so that no one who's been daydreaming thinks he's in trouble.

You can insert students' names into sentences you use for grammar lessons, into math story problems, and into examples of scientific research. ("Calvin was showing symptoms of sleeping sickness; he was dozing off while on the soccer field, and his teammates were getting concerned . . .")

# Play with a bit of old-fashioned competition.

Like spelling bees. You can have math bees, geography bees, government bees . . . Choose teams at random; no stacking of the deck allowed. And if one team is lagging far behind another, you might throw out a freebie, a question so easy that even a three-year-old could answer it. Or else interject one totally off the subject ("Explain the principle behind mixing an effective pesticide"), then recover and mumble, "Oops! Wrong list."

This is also an excellent way to build cooperation. You'll need to decide whether to make those team rosters permanent or occasionally juggle them. How to choose? Study what's taking place. Is the competition good natured—or cutthroat? Is someone strutting too much? If so, a change may be in order.

# Shower your kids with applause and affection.

No, I don't mean the physical kind. When someone gives a supremely complete and correct answer, go berserk with joy. It could be the best memory someone has of the entire year—especially if the class learns to join in.

Pump your arms or raise them toward heaven in gratitude, do an Irish jig, and shout, "YESSS!" The more exaggerated, the better. It's not the same as phony, contrived praise; it's a comedy skit, which everyone enjoys.

# Stretch minds.

At least once a month, schedule a "story" half-hour. Take a chapter from history or an aspect of science or technology that they're unlikely to hear about until years later, and relate it in an easy-to-follow, soap opera fashion. You want everyone sitting on the edges of their seats.

A few historical suggestions: Henry VIII's procession of six wives. The Salem witch trials. Marie Antoinette's rampant consumerism as the masses starved. The insane Russian monk, Rasputin. The Lindbergh baby's kidnapping. JFK's assassination. The 1986 *Challenger* explosion—with a teacher on board.

Scientific or technological options: early methods of medical intervention, such as bloodletting and the use of leeches and maggots. The mysteries involved in constructing the pyramids of Egypt and the circular formation at Stonehenge (some authorities once suggested that extraterrestrials assisted with both).

# End every class period with a teaser.

"Wait till you hear what Hamlet says to his girlfriend, Ophelia. You'll want to smack him!"

"You aren't going to believe what happens to Lincoln's wife, Mary, following his death!"

"Guess how many baby goslings a mother cares for at one time!"

# Impress upon your students again and again that from you they can always expect unusual lessons.

How to do this? By being lovably eccentric, but stopping just short of weird. A sharp intellect, an inquiring mind, and a quick wit are all helpful. You must, however, do this within a consistent, predictable structure—which all children crave. So you'll need to strike a balance, where your private personality is calm and soothing, while your public performance is dynamic and entertaining.

You'll know you've been successful when you see your kids entering your room with little bounces in their steps.

# Specific Suggestions for Specific Subjects

## Math

**You'd better be talking about money— constantly!** How else do you think students will use math in real life? By balancing their checkbooks, calculating how much that new car will really cost with interest, deciding whether it's cheaper to fly to Florida out of Cincinnati or Dayton. How many square yards of new carpeting does a bedroom need? How much interest are you paying each year on your credit card? What does 1/4 cup of sugar look like? You get the idea.

**Refer often to resources like Suze Orman's *Guide to Wealth* and Robert Kiyosaki's *Rich Dad, Poor Dad*.** Let the class decide over time which ones deliver the goods and which ones are more hype than results. One of my favorites is *The Trick to Money Is Having Some*, by Stuart Wilde. Wilde preaches intention, detachment, and spiritual abundance—but unlike many of his coterie, he will leave you debating issues far into the night. Example: a fair price is anything that two or more people agree on. Really?

**Designate Monday as "Let's All Get Rich" day and Friday as "Let's Buy Something Cool" day—but can we afford it?** Mondays are for learning about investing. Fridays are for looking at used-car dealerships and extended warranties on flat-screen TVs.

# History

## Pose hypotheticals.
How would you behave if your city or state were occupied by a foreign government? Use individuals (with their consent) as examples: What would Robbie do if his family were told they had to feed and quarter three Iranian militants at their own expense? American colonists were forced to house British soldiers!

## Remind students that it's unfair to judge 1790 behavior by 2009 standards. However . . .
What kinds of deeds that are commonplace today might be considered morally bankrupt in the future? Medical testing on animals, perhaps? Government's seizing of private homes to build new roads and shopping malls, otherwise known as eminent domain? Treating health care as a profit-driven privilege rather than a right?

# Science

## Get your class's attention by grossing them out.
Ask five kids to spit into paper cups so you can find out what's really in saliva; then ask one guy to collect all of the cups. And while you're at it, why does urine smell like ammonia?

## Continually refer to three things that are always fascinating about animals: reproduction, parenting habits, and their similarities to humans.
And how do humans stack up against them in terms of altruism versus aggression and greed?

## Initiate ethical debates.
Is nuclear energy preferable to utility company monopolies? Are flu pandemics inevitable? Have we already missed the boat on global warming?

# Government

Ask students to list what they consider the most essential laws for a civilized society. Then ask them to list what governments should stay out of. Challenge their thinking with plenty of what-ifs. Those of us from the idealistic 1960s can offer an interesting perspective: Why did our original plans for peace and international goodwill fail? How did things fly so far off course?

Ask for input on everything from Social Security to the current health care crisis—backed up with plenty of independent research. It's their world now. They'll have to live in it longer than we will. They can't afford to be apathetic.

# Literature

**Remember that characters, although perhaps imaginary, do reflect real behavior and are often mirrored in our own lives.** Many lessons can be learned from fictional characters found in literature and films. One thought: post somewhere in your classroom a line from *Shadowlands,* the movie about the writer C. S. Lewis:

> " We read to know that we're not alone. "

Your students can relate to Jay Gatsby, whose adoration of Daisy disintegrates when he discovers how shallow she really is.

To Jane Eyre, who sees beyond Mr. Rochester's angry, cynical defense, and grows to loves him, even after she learns the truth about the madwoman hidden in the attic.

To Romeo and Juliet, those star-crossed lovers who, through death, teach their families and friends to move beyond hate and violence.

> " Abstract themes of literature grow out of the pain of ordinary people and need to be studied, not for critical exercise, but for their capacity to heal. "
>
> **—JOAN CUTULY**

# 8

## Classroom Management —Otherwise Known as Discipline

*"Teachers are among the few managers who must deal with workers who are disruptive."*
**—William Glasser**

# The disciplinary conundrum is still educational rocket science.

Meaning that it's the most complex issue any teacher ever faces.

No matter how dedicated and dynamic you are, it does no good whatsoever if your classes won't settle down long enough to listen to you. Yet instruction on how to handle a roomful of young people is still sketchy at best. Education classes often spend far too little time on the thorny topic of classroom management. One possible reason? There are so few absolutes. It's a science with huge amounts of art thrown in—and therefore to a large extent, *unteachable*.

Most of us learn our most effective techniques, in fact, through observation, along with plenty of painful trial and error.

It has always been thus. Even one-room schoolhouses had plenty of young "rowdies" who kept their teachers constantly on edge. And if you crave a more recent yet still historical example, rent the 1955 film *The Blackboard Jungle*, starring Glenn Ford as a hapless teacher, and Sidney Poitier, who was actually twenty-eight, as a high school student. Today's problems may be far more complicated than they were back then, but misbehaving schoolchildren have always been—and will always be—with us.

Please keep in mind, though, that 99 percent of your problems will be caused by only about 2 percent of your students. The vast majority will never give you an ounce of trouble. It's that other (smaller) group that will drive you batty. You'll also notice a complete climate shift whenever one of your disruptive influences is absent.

Ideally, you'd like to pursue a successful teaching career without a single disciplinary incident. Sorry. That won't happen. You may be fortunate enough to have low numbers, but nobody gets away with none. Nobody.

What's more, student behavior is unpredictable. One class will give you its full, respectful attention from day one. Another is so antsy that it seems borrowed from Bedlam, the British insane asylum the operated for centuries whose name has become synonymous with chaos.

You may never understand why you become a class target. It has absolutely nothing to do with your age, size, gender, or degree of attractiveness. Old teachers, young teachers, males and females, 230-pound former linebackers and 90-pound former cheerleaders—we all get more than our share.

Here's the dilemma: whether or not you seem in charge and hence *unshakable* depends on one thing: your physical presence, which takes time to develop.

As a first-year teacher, I was fortunate enough to discover early on that I didn't have the drill sergeant archetype anywhere inside me. Try as I might to locate him (some of my early memories of barking orders are truly comical; former students still tease me at class reunions), he just wasn't in there.

So I switched gears. It was a difficult process, with plenty of setbacks. After all, I'd been trained by the "Don't Smile Until Christmas" generation of mentors. But the kinder, gentler approach eventually won out. Now I can look back and declare proudly that my number of discipline problems over thirty-one years was relatively small.

And what's more, I'm about to unveil all of my secrets. You may not agree with everything I have to say. That's fine. Adopt what's useful. Toss the rest.

Let's start with a few foundational insights.

# Control over your class isn't really the issue; ultimately we control only ourselves.

In other words, if you find ways to make your classes *want* to behave, to make acting out an exercise in futility, then you're pretty much home free. Sounds simple, doesn't it? It's not. Finding the delicate balance between high standards and friendly goodwill involves a huge web of interconnected strategies that can take years to fine-tune but that eventually become so instinctive and automatic that you can't even list the ingredients.

For now, know this: externally imposed discipline is a mere stopgap. The only kind that lasts is the kind that comes from inside. We must model for our kids how to find that—and how good it feels when we do.

> You cannot 'make' your students work hard. In fact, if what you do is not satisfying, you cannot even 'make' yourself work hard.
> **—WILLIAM GLASSER**

# Everyone would rather be a success than a failure.

It's a trait inborn in every human organism. Given a choice, every student would prefer to graduate from Harvard than hang out on a street corner. So why doesn't he? Easy. He doesn't believe it's possible.

It's your job to help him find his way. No, not to graduate from Harvard; in the majority of cases, that's unrealistic—but maybe to earn an authentic high school diploma (rather than a GED), which is, for many, still an uphill climb.

You're unlikely to accomplish that by becoming a drill sergeant.

There are two ways to govern: by fear and intimidation, or by kindness, concern, and encouragement. The first, not unlike a dictatorship, sows the seeds of rebellion. The second allows the student to make his own choices, but also to save face when he makes inappropriate ones.

Every hard-core discipline case I ever encountered became one, I believe, because someone somewhere had convinced him (or he'd convinced himself) that academic achievement was not an option. Becoming the worst kid in school carried far more status than being a nobody. No wonder so many labor so hard year after year to attain such exalted notoriety!

Yet you truly have the power to pull someone back from that brink.

# Nearly all of your disciplinary problems will be due to one of two things: anger or boredom.

Does that amaze you? It should. Many people believe that troublesome kids are just plain mean. Not so.

First, anger. How would you feel about having to report every morning for several years to a place you hate, wasting your time in a demanding but nonpaying job that basically amounts to indentured servitude, being lorded over by supervisors who not only fill your brain with useless information but also delight in writing out detention slips to make you stay late—and then, even worse, tell you what you can and can't wear and make you feel slow and foolish in the process?

I certainly disagreed when my students described school as a prison, but I also understood why they called it that. Many of my vocational kids had full-time professional employment waiting for them as soon as they could break free. Quite a compelling offer: dignity *and* money! But to earn a diploma, they had to stay in my room for another three to nine months. Bummer.

What they didn't realize was that their anger was the real prison. Some kids were so entrapped in so many layers of rage that they weren't even aware of how it all started. (Talking about this openly in class, particularly exploring some ways to regain a bit of power and control, helped a great deal.)

Second, boredom. By now you've sat through your share of in-service days, where you listen for hours to some "expert" telling you how to do your job better. At 4:00 P.M. you drive home semiconscious and then collapse, more exhausted than on any other day of the year. Well, multiply that by 180.

Listening is hard work, especially when the talk is about something on which you place no value. Boredom soon turns to anger.

The toughest class I ever had was a group of seniors, engineering design technology students—bright, bright, bright—but still categorized as vocational, because the course was part of the overall program. I was therefore saddled with required resource materials that wouldn't have challenged the average fifth grader. You know, "How to write a friendly letter," that sort of thing.

Eventually, after a few short weeks and getting to know how incredible this class really was, I explained the problem to an understanding vocational coordinator, then began writing my own lesson plans, depending less and less on those evil loose-leaf notebooks stacked on the radiator. But it was too late. The kids were already furious at me for having demeaned them by insulting their intelligence. And they were right. However unwittingly, I had.

At the start of the second semester I finally came clean, admitted what had taken place, and promised to do better. The discipline problems disappeared, but I was left with a group sitting mostly in stoic silence and refusing to participate in any class discussions. They were still mad as hornets—and the only person they could see fit to blame was me.

Not a pleasant memory.

The following year was better—I began on the first day with my own materials and wound up with one of the most affectionate, outspoken, endearing classes of my entire career. But I still feel terrible about that earlier bunch.

Boredom is the absolute kiss of death. So check not only your lesson plans but also your delivery. If you're saddled with dull, unimaginative material or prone to long-winded, monotonous speeches, then you're literally torturing your students. Sort of like the teacher played by the brilliant Ben Stein in *Ferris Bueller's Day Off*.

For which you will pay dearly.

# As a teacher, you're a disciplinary sitting duck.

Yes, you. The person who has devoted his or her life to making life better for others.

There isn't a kid walking who doesn't know you're a handy target for all his frustration—because you can't fight back. You're a professional; you're not allowed to descend into sarcasm or name-calling. Only he is. So not only can he spew whatever vitriol he pleases, but he can then complain to his parents that you're "picking" on him, take his case all the way to the front office, and probably have any punishment you decide to inflict lowered or even rescinded.

This grants students an awesome license. And they know it.

But all is not lost. The remedy is to take yourself completely out of the fray. You'll see how shortly.

> "If you believe that old techniques would work if people would just act the way they used to, you already have a discipline problem difficult to solve."
> —**JIM FAY AND DAVID FUNK**

# Kids and adults are not equals—but society has taught them that they are.

One of the more irritating traits among many of today's teenagers is that they truly believe they should have the same rights and privileges as we do. Smoking, drinking, driving, keeping odd hours, consuming goods and services, leaving class or skipping school whenever they feel like it . . . all without paying property taxes or utility bills, or assuming any responsibility whatsoever for keeping a household (or community) running. An added perk: being permitted to challenge all authority, regardless of what rule they've been caught violating.

That's why you may hear, "Well, it's his word against yours," when you send a student to the office. Sputtering indignation will not save you. The scales of justice between teacher and student are not even. The only way to rebalance them is through detailed records and a story that does not change, no matter how many times you are asked to retell it.

# Parents have tunnel vision.

As they should. Their concern focuses in only one direction—their child. Is she getting a generous portion of your time and attention? Are you doing everything you can to stimulate and encourage her?

Are you being fair?

I remind you of this only because disciplinary altercations where parents are called in can easily result in guns blazing. But there's plenty you can do to diffuse that. Act delighted to meet them. Ask a few questions: Where do they work? How many other kids do they have? Then mention something positive you've witnessed about little Barry. Then bring up the concern. Lean forward. Keep your voice soft, mellow, sympathetic. Propose a solution. Promise to stay in touch. Let them know the very moment you see any behavioral improvement.

# The biggest problem schools face isn't what you think it is.

It really isn't discipline. It's apathy.

Sometimes that apathy is evident in a high truancy rate. Once the courts got involved and began fining (and confining!) parents when their offspring repeatedly refused to show up, things got better. But we still have our share of cases where moms drop kids off dutifully at the school's front door and then drive away, only to have those same kids stroll out the back and head for the nearest fast-food joint.

Other parents are very much part of the problem. They think it's perfectly okay to keep a kid home from school because he has a sore toe or needs to catch up on his sleep, or because (unbelievably) his favorite baseball team is in town playing a home game.

Anyway, silence is not necessarily golden. Kids who act out are easier to reach than kids who have shut down. Acting out at least means that some degree of caring is still present! This is a person who can still be reached by a teacher who's willing to take on the mission. Gee, think what could happen if we only had more dedicated manpower.

# What constitutes insubordination is highly subjective.

There will be some incidents that you'll feel foolish even reporting because they sound so ridiculous.

For example: I asked a girl (politely, I thought) to stop chatting and get busy with her class work. To my astonishment, she closed her eyes in annoyance and gave me several dismissive waves of her hand. I was flabbergasted—and I wasn't the only one. Gasps of shock and disbelief rippled through the entire room. This was by far the most insulting, revolting, demeaning thing that had ever happened to me as a teacher.

But I tell you, I had one heck of a time communicating that to the girl's administrator. It was like, "Let me get this straight. You're upset because she *waved* at you?" (No, she waved me *away*.)

Polish your writing skills, and don't hesitate to add words like "insulting," "revolting," and "demeaning." This kind of contempt and disrespect cannot and should not be ignored.

# In-school suspension is a brilliant concept. So is alternative school.

Long ago, a kid who'd racked up a whole series of offenses was suspended, then sent home for three or five or ten days to think things over. One problem was that upon his return, he was permitted to make up his work, which meant that Guess Who was required to sit with him after school and on her own time. Which meant the equivalent of a paid vacation for the culprit, as said makeup work was an abbreviated, condensed version of what had been covered that week in class and required lots of teacher guidance.

Finally somebody decided it was a better idea to suspend students from classes, not from school. It also kept kids off the streets, something both parents and retailers appreciated.

The alternative school is also a recent development, a product of our realization that there are some kids who simply aren't suited to the traditional school environment. This is an express lane of sorts, where one teacher guides his or her group through basic material and offers plenty of individualized attention.

It's easy to dismiss both concepts as catering to recalcitrant brats who refuse to conform. But having visited both sites, I have to tell you that they work extremely well—and I believe that they keep a lot of teens in school who would otherwise drop out. It's a compromise, but a justifiable one.

# For kids, so much suffering—hence, misbehavior—comes from feeling stupid and inept.

The most damaging thing a teacher can do is to make a kid feel dumb. Yet we often do exactly that with our demands and our commands and our inflexibility and our high standards. Hear me on this: you can't cure the agony of misbehavior or underachievement with punishments.

Imagine being told that you must learn Russian, starting today. There will be a vocabulary test in one week—and, by golly, you'd better be ready! One learning expert says that the American public school system's message to students often sounds like this: "We can't save you from drowning until after you take swimming lessons." In other words, learn the material first. Then we'll try to work with you.

He also says that taking longer than three seconds to answer a question in class is deemed unacceptable. So kids are rarely granted enough time to connect any dots. Math or geography class turns into a game show like *Jeopardy*. For every wrong answer, the stakes are high—chastisement and humiliation. What no one tells you is that ten to fifteen seconds of "wait" time can make a huge difference.

Make a kid feel stupid, and he'll find a way to get even. Or else he'll write himself off and withdraw. After all, if he doesn't try, then he can't lose. Either way, he may fall through the cracks and become another statistic.

**"** Praise youth and it will prosper. **"**
**—IRISH PROVERB**

# Your ultimate challenge, then, is to give each student what he wants and needs, yet still retain your own authority and integrity.

What does he need? Success. The knowledge that he can pass your class and earn his credit. What else? Dignity and self-esteem, the sense that he's respected as a person, even if you two are addressing each other across a cultural gulf as wide as the Grand Canyon—as you often will be.

The so-called self-esteem movement failed, we now realize, because it was built on a foundation of telling a child he was wonderful just because he happened to exist. True self-esteem, we know now, comes from accomplishment.

What does he want? Some fun along the way. Luckily, all of this is within his reach, because it's also within yours.

> Don't laugh at a youth for his affectations; he is only trying on one face after another to find his own.
> **—LOGAN PEARSALL SMITH**

# 9

# Tricky Strategies All Teachers Can Master

*They may like you, they may even love you, but they are young, and it is the business of the young to push the old off the planet. If you hang on, you learn the tricks.*

**—Frank McCourt**

# Never disrupt your own lesson.

You're talking, talking, and Jake is rhythmically rapping a pencil against his seat. Or Monica is braiding Selena's hair. Or Sally is painting her fingernails.

Don't say a word. Don't break stride. Keep talking, stroll over, and place a gentle hand on top of the culprit's. Give it a light pat to signal that you're not angry.

Or Bruce is happily sketching gargoyles on his desktop. You keep talking, stroll over to your closet, grab a bottle of spray cleaner and a paper towel, then place it gently on Bruce's desk. And give him too an affectionate shoulder pat. Continue as if nothing had occurred.

You may hear a few chuckles, but you haven't really lost anyone's attention; in fact, you've probably gained it.

> Most good teachers find a way to deliver the skills without reducing classrooms to boot camps.
> **—JONATHAN KOZOL**

# Know your own hot buttons—and then communicate them.

Kids spend a great deal of time trying to figure out what will make their teachers explode—and then take fiendish pleasure in causing that to happen. So eliminate the game. Tell them, "This is what makes me crazy. Don't do it, or I will not be able to cut you a break when you need it."

Want an example? Many teachers go ballistic over gum chewing. It never particularly bothered me. When I spotted it, I just placed the wastebasket nearest the kid(s) who were chomping away. This increased the chances of said gum finding its way into the trash at period's end. If it didn't make it, I had more important stuff to worry about.

In contrast, two things that drove me nuts were sleeping and doing other homework in my class. Early in the year, I stated clearly, "If I catch you doing your math, I'll remove both paper and book, and you'll have to call your lawyer to get them back." Occasionally someone would violate the edict, I'd do exactly as promised, and even nearby classmates would sigh and say, "Oh, man, how idiotic can you be?"

Ah, peer pressure can be so reinforcing.

As for sleepers, see the next page.

# Carry a camera.

I only began doing this in desperation during the final five years, but it was extremely effective. Anytime anyone fell asleep, I snapped her picture. (After all, they'd all been warned.) Then I sent one copy to her guidance counselor and posted the other on my bulletin board. If the comatose culprit got prickly, I promised to take it down after she'd stayed awake for five days running. Sounded fair enough.

In these days of digital cameras, you'll get away cheaper than I did with my double prints at Walgreens. You can e-mail counselors and, if in a particularly sinister mood, parents too.

Seriously, the primary cause of this constant passing out on desktops is part-time jobs, which really amount to full-time. I had students working forty to fifty hours in addition to attending class. Ridiculous—but not something over which I had any control. I would therefore make it as inconvenient as possible for that to continue. If nothing else, I had ready proof for Mom and Dad that no schoolwork was taking place—due to the fact that in each photo, the kid was wearing a completely different shirt.

But when confronted by a student, I turned instantly kind and concerned: "Sure would hate to see you lose this credit. You'd have to sit through my class again next year and feel like you're watching reruns. So how about keeping your eyes open?"

# Get in touch with your inner child—it's the key to your style.

I'm a baby boomer, raised in the 1950s—and contrary to what you've read, most of us back then weren't particularly pampered or indulged. Our parents were Depression-era children and therefore from the "We ate dirt and were glad to have it on our plates" school of thought. So some of their punishments were what we would today consider . . . well, abusive.

Spanking aside, the worst part of being a 1950s kid was the assumption that whatever you did wrong was the result of being intentionally sneaky and mean-spirited. How was I to know at age five that my father wouldn't appreciate having the inside of his garage painted seven different colors?

I was the kind of child who learned best when reprimanded gently—and it took only one time. Occasionally that happened, but more often lessons were learned by way of a very hard paddle. Talk about overkill!

As a teacher, I learned to spot which kids were cut from similar cloth. I would take them aside and speak very softly. They would smile and nod. The problem would instantly disappear. The funny thing was, the longer I spent in education, the more kids I encountered who responded well to that method. Soon it seemed as if nearly everyone did. When my own children arrived, I used the same technique. Throughout even their teenage years, we never had a single incident of grounding or a single slammed door.

If you too were a shy, eager-to-please child, you'll encounter plenty of little kindred spirits, even in teenage bodies. Act accordingly.

# Get off your behind.

You cannot teach a class effectively by sitting at your desk. The body language screams "Barrier!" You must be up and moving around the perimeter. Your physical proximity will eliminate a lot of whispering, note passing, shrugging, and eyeball rolling.

You can, however, sit atop your desk. You're still visible, accessible, friendly. Many of my students found the prowling up and down rows, which most classroom management courses heartily recommend, intimidating. So I did very little of it. Gauge your climate and study those faces.

# Treat some insensitive comments as jokes.

There you are, chugging along, teaching what you think is a pretty good lesson, and you mention how frustrating it is to work so hard on a plan and then arrive to see half your class absent.

"Well," some smart-mouth in the third row remarks, "it wouldn't happen if your topics weren't so boring."

What you'd like to do is pretend that his head is a soccer ball.

What you should do instead is clutch your chest in a mock heart attack and moan loudly in pain. If you can manage it, fall against a chair. Everyone laughs, including you, and the tense moment is over. You emerge as a hero with a great sense of humor.

I'm also a huge fan of "the look," the one that instantly means, "Stop whatever you're doing"—except I favor making it a total caricature, so monstrous and malevolent that everyone can't help chuckling. A Halloween mask helps, if you're quick enough to retrieve it from your desk drawer.

# Hold one-on-one conferences.

Yes, while students are working at their seats. You'll be sorely tempted to use that precious time to grade papers. Don't do it. You've got bigger fish to fry. Like getting to know each and every kid as an individual. Every personal relationship you forge means one less disciplinary problem.

Maybe your (short) talk will be about his grades. Maybe it will be about his personal life. Don't dictate. Begin with "How's it going?" and see where things lead. If all you get is silence, try again the following week.

Some teachers have successfully made lunch "dates" with their students. (Teacher buys.) Do it only if you (and they) feel totally comfortable alone in your classroom. (Door wide open.) I knew one guy who twice a week plopped down with his lunch tray at a full table of his math students. I admired his courage. He was one of the most respected teachers in the building.

But always keep it cool. No pressure. Start by chatting about nothing. It will turn into something.

# Check all criticism: Is it really constructive?

Sad to say, it rarely is. People who begin by saying, "I'm telling you this for your own good" hardly ever are. They just like feeling in charge. So stifle all impulses to offer unsolicited advice.

Try this instead: "I have some feedback. Would you like to hear it?"

Nearly everyone will say yes. If someone doesn't, accept it with grace. Maybe her curiosity will get the better of her.

> Never give advice unless asked.
> **—GERMAN PROVERB**

# Give your students regular pep talks.

Start like this: "What I love about your generation is . . ." You can say this with a straight face even if you are from the same generation. When you became a teacher, you instantly hopped that fence.

Keep a running list. Pull from it constantly. Here are a few samples to get you started:

They have political opinions.

They are generally well informed regarding current events.

They don't consider volunteer work beneath them.

They read. They have favorite books.

They aren't particularly gullible regarding scam artists.

They are all, without exception, computer literate.

Don't laugh at some of my obvious choices. Kids need to hear good things about themselves.

My senior social studies teacher in 1964 was one of the smartest men in the world. But he would browbeat us with his opinions and commentaries. And one of his favorite subjects was one we titled behind his back, "You Rotten Kids . . ."

He would spend entire class periods putting us down for everything from not knowing much about history to still depending on our parents for weekly allowances. His voice virtually dripped with sarcasm. And in those days we didn't dare answer back. We just sat there, feeling utterly hopeless and miserable.

# Use hidden flattery to ratchet goals and expectations.

"Anyone as smart as you already knows that . . ."

"You have far too much integrity to take part in . . ."

"It wouldn't be fair to your ability level to let you slide on . . ."

I know it sounds terribly manipulative, but as long as you aren't just blowing smoke, I see no reason why you shouldn't focus on a student's best qualities to encourage him or her to reach higher. Who doesn't bask with delight in someone else's admiration?

# Cultivate class jokes.

It's the key to camaraderie. Someone utters a single word or phrase, and everyone erupts into laughter—and an observer is sitting there looking like, "Huh?"

Just be certain that the joke isn't at the expense of any student. It can, however, be at yours—in fact, that's much safer ground.

An example: one year I took my vocational seniors to the art museum. (A whole tale in itself.) As we exited, I looked around and inquired, "Where's the bus?" Everyone busted up; it was parked right in front of me. From then on, every time anyone wasn't paying attention in class, someone else would say, "Where's the bus?" A lighthearted moment often replaced what might have turned into a disciplinary confrontation.

Another example: in 1990, I tacked a Woodstock poster on my bulletin board. It was a crowd scene—hundreds of beaded, bearded longhairs and hot chicks from 1969 cheering a rock band. My kids loved it; they were fascinated by Woodstock anyway (three days of peace and love) and were captivated by my stories about being a teenager in the 1960s.

One day a student approached me and said, "Paul Jenkins is on that poster." I looked—and sure enough, one face in the crowd was a dead ringer for someone in my fourth-period class! I grabbed a pen and wrote "Paul Jenkins" on that kid's T-shirt. Soon everyone was gathered around the bulletin board, pointing out other amazing resemblances. And pulling out pens.

This went on for several years. The T-shirts filled up. Each semester we discovered more and more clones. That poster became a sort of icon throughout the entire school and a reason for kids I didn't even know to drop by for a look. Those whose names got labeled paraded around like celebrities. "Did you know I was at Woodstock? Look. Here's proof." It was hilarious.

But also a great way to teach my students that teenagers are teenagers, regardless of the era.

> Jokes of the proper kind, properly told, can do more to enlighten questions of politics, philosophy, and literature than any number of dull arguments.
>
> —ISAAC ASIMOV

# Never lose your temper.

Okay, you will—but let's hope it happens only once, because you will feel like a complete idiot afterward. Why? Because deep down you already know that you're never more out of control than when you are yelling at someone. And the more pompous and bullying you sound, the more your insecurity and fear are showing.

Even worse, the kids know it. They consider this the greatest show on Earth.

So force yourself to go into the hall and take a couple of deep breaths. When you return, tell your class you'll discuss the issue later when you are calmer. This may involve sending the kid who caused the explosion to the office. Do so quietly, with dignity.

> " I am extraordinarily patient, provided I get my own way in the end. "
> —**MARGARET THATCHER**

# Never hold a grudge.

Every day should be a fresh start. The kids are allowed to fold their arms, pout, and act snotty. You're not. You're the adult.

Late in my career, though, I noticed a strange dynamic. After I'd read Dr. Deborah Tannen's work on male and female conversation patterns, I realized that whenever I had a disciplinary altercation with a boy, it was often the first, last, and only incident. With a girl, in contrast, it could be just the beginning of a whole semester's worth of baiting on her part. Strange.

But Tannen claimed this was mirrored in boys' playground clashes. One could beat up another, and then later they'd wind up playing on the same basketball team. Girls rarely did that. What was reflected in my classroom, then, was a version of the same male pattern: battle over, victor declared, no more reason to challenge. It made sense. I eventually published an article about it in *English Journal*.

Girls were tougher to win over. I eventually discovered that my best strategy after we'd clashed was a sudden bout of amnesia. Each day thereafter I greeted them as warmly as if no conflict had ever occurred. In time, most softened. I recall only one case where it took the entire year—but then, on the last day of school, she actually wrote me a thank-you note.

# Don't be afraid to apologize.

If you're wrong, that is. It may take place right away with an entire group, or a day later with a single student. Don't worry about losing respect; you'll gain it instead. Particularly if you employ what I call the "power" apology, where you retain your grace and dignity and then stress what you, rather than someone else, did that was inappropriate.

Granted, it's a tough act—but it gets easier with practice. And the impression you make can last a lifetime.

Once a boy named Eddie turned in a research paper that was a complete disaster. That wasn't unusual; he was in a class of low-level juniors who'd never written one before. I'd even built time for rewrites into the project, knowing that few would get it right on their first attempt. But Eddie's was such a mess that I threw up my hands in frustration, saying, "Looks like you'll be attending summer school to earn your credit."

That night after I went home, it hit me that at least he'd tried. And the work was definitely his. Unlike, I suspected, a couple of others in the class.

I called Eddie immediately and told him I'd reacted too hastily and that we'd talk about a do-over the next day. I'm sure he slept well that night. I certainly did.

# Always leave the back door open.

Never confront or try to humiliate a student in front of his peers. He will get himself expelled before he allows you to make him look a fool.

So much of avoiding bad scenes is leaving the disciplinary door open a crack just large enough for a student to scuttle through. You get what you want: the problem goes away. He gets what he wants: he saves face.

Sometimes it involves offering a choice: "You can either get busy here in class, or you'll need to take that work home tonight."

Sometimes it involves a reinforcing comment: "Dawn Marie is just using me for practice—she opens this Saturday night at the Comedy Club."

Sometimes it involves doing something out of the ordinary. When a student crossed the line of good-natured kidding into something that felt less positive, or when he simply wouldn't stop interrupting me, I'd ask him to step outside into the hall. The class fell silent and motionless; they were eager to overhear a showdown. They never got one. Once outside I'd say, "Let's both take a deep breath," or "You know what I'm going to say, don't you? Good. Then I don't need to say it." And we'd go back inside.

It was often like pressing the restart button on a computer.

# Act "as if."

In other words, if you don't care for a particular student, you absolutely must fake it. There's no justification for not liking a kid and letting it show. You must become the world's greatest actor.

Oddly, in some cases, once you've pretended long enough, you may find something slightly endearing about the little mutt.

> "I love acting. It is so much more real than life."
> —OSCAR WILDE

# Go after your dropouts.

Do it by phone, e-mail, or perhaps even a home visit. Home visits are actually pretty cool; you get to see how a kid fits into the family structure, you meet Mom and Dad, even the little brother who will be in your class in about five years.

When a kid drops out, he's usually convinced that no one will miss him. Reassure him that someone will. Tell him he's welcome to return . . . whenever. Offer your business card in case he decides he wants to talk. You may leave convinced that because the student is probably not coming back, it's time badly spent. You'll be wrong. That kid and his family will remember your face at their kitchen table for the rest of their lives.

# Cultivate at least one student relationship outside your specialty.

Study halls are good for this. Occasionally even hall duty.

Because I specialized in underachievers, many of whom were smart but unmotivated, it was always eye-opening when I got close to one of those jet-propelled movers and shakers. A thirty-year-old trapped inside a sixteen-year-old body. A kid who was absolutely certain that one day he'd become President. It reaffirmed my faith in the next generation times ten. After a chat with one of them, I could feel my own energy level soaring.

But before I could start feeling sorry for myself and my own demanding class load, their teachers reminded me that staying a week ahead of them could be even more exhausting than my own efforts to keep my groups awake.

Once when I was assigned to be sophomore class sponsor, we had a school dance where we wound up with two rather than the one required policeman. The reason? The class president had assumed that it was his duty to line one up. I had assumed that it was mine. I wasn't accustomed to kids who accepted responsibilities without nagging.

So we happily paid both cops out of the dance's proceeds—and then the four of us "adults" spent the whole evening laughing about how Bryan should think about running for mayor.

# Good cop–bad cop still works.

In case you're not familiar with the terminology, it operates like this: when the police bring in a suspect, the first cop hammers him with berating, shouting, threats, and accusations. Suspect clams up, shuts down. The second cop saunters in with take-out food and hot coffee, apologizes for the antics of his partner, befriends the suspect . . . who, within an atmosphere of "caring," spills a confession.

This can be useful in schools too, when two hall monitors are trying to find out who just set off the fire alarm.

But there's another level to consider. I was once fortunate enough to have an assistant principal who insisted he had to stick to the rules without exception. In public, that is. Behind closed doors he was delighted to let me plead a kid's case and "convince" him that the student deserved a second chance. He'd then growl to the kid that only his teacher's concern and intervention on his behalf had saved the day. A little shady? Sure. But it often changed a miserable attitude about school forever.

And the real hero, in my mind, was that assistant principal willing to be cast in the role of bad cop in order to make that happen.

# Ditto, love-children.

I'm talking about the occasions when an administrator or fellow teacher and I happened to share a mutual affection for a student who had a propensity for getting into trouble. We'd greet each other in the hallway with "How's our boy today?" "A little restless; handle him carefully." Or perhaps: "Can I keep him for an extra period? I think he'll settle down if I let him clean off some desks while we talk."

It was another assistant principal who christened one such case "our love-child," and it still makes me grin.

# Practice these lines.

**"I can't hear Bob."** Used during class discussions when everyone is talking at once and you want to return the floor to the person who was interrupted. No one feels disrespected when you treat one student's opinion as important as your own.

**"What will help me understand you better?"** Used one-on-one with a student who doesn't seem to be doing (or behaving) well.

**"I'll think about it and let you know."** Used when you're asked to make an exception that doesn't feel instantly comfortable. You may just need to tweak it a bit.

**"I admire the way you handled that."** Used when you observe someone reacting to a wiseacre remark with dignity.

**"How's that workin' for ya?"** Borrowed from Dr. Phil. Used when a student is trying to justify bad or foolish behavior.

**"I see you have decided to . . ."** Borrowed from Dr. Haim Ginott, author of *Between Teacher and Child*. Used to put the power of choice back on the student's own shoulders.

**"Who wants me to make his life a total misery?"** This began as a joke with second-semester seniors who were in danger of not receiving their diplomas. I told them (tongue in cheek, or so I thought) I was perfectly willing to nag and harass them into getting their work done. Hands shot up! Volunteers everywhere! So I created a signup sheet and posted it on the bulletin board. Scrawled remarks ranged from "Yes, please!" to "Give it to me!" What might have been the usual spring tug-of-war became instead a source of constant laughter until their graduation ceremony in June.

# Pass notes.

You to them. Keeping a kid after class can be embarrassing for her, even if you don't have an ax to grind. So put your concern in writing: "Connie—I've noticed you haven't handed in your theme yet. What's going on? Let me know."

This is especially useful if behavior is an ongoing worry: "Jack—You seem so unhappy in my class. Would you like me to see the guidance counselor about a transfer?" That line was often enough for the student to object, "No, I like it here; I'm having other problems." Sometimes to my surprise this resulted in a regular correspondence back and forth. In several instances, handwritten notes were pressed into my hand almost daily as students entered and left my room.

Remember, when writing, that you are always concerned, not superior. Having a teacher in your face should be a welcome thing, not a reason to turn defensive.

# Beware the nonapology.

Occasionally you'll encounter a counselor or principal who believes that the ultimate solution to every infraction is for the student to apologize to the teacher. I don't disagree with the philosophy so much as the practice. Too often you'll hear, "I don't think I did nothin' wrong, man, but if you think I did, I guess I apologize."

That's not a far leap from the convicted felon who declares to an aggrieved family whose grandfather he beat and robbed, "I'm sorry if I hurt anyone." If? Or worse: "I'm sorry about what happened." It didn't just "happen"; he committed a heinous crime.

Trust your gut. If you feel as if a second bucket of mud just got dumped on your head, then don't accept the nonapology. Say, "I'm sorry, but I'm not feeling the love here. Try again, and make it real this time."

# Beware the "good kid" line.

I must have heard it a dozen times from parents of students who were habitually disrespectful. Were these moms and dads blind and deaf? No. Read between the lines. "He's really a good kid" secretly means "I'm really a good parent."

Don't argue. There are egos at stake here. Respond by saying, "Yes, but he made a bad choice. We need to be sure that never happens again."

# There's always another chance to turn things around—always.

It's the last day of school. You're sitting at your desk, feverishly grading exams, swilling down tepid coffee, when you hear a tap at your door. The knob turns—and there stands your nemesis, the kid who just spent an entire year sabotaging your carefully crafted lessons.

He tiptoes forward. "I just want to say," he ventures, "that I'm sorry I caused so much trouble. You're really a very good teacher."

You try to be gracious, but a part of you remains stiff-lipped. Why couldn't he have found this level of maturity and empathy nine months earlier?

Because he wasn't ready yet. And now he is.

And you were instrumental in fostering that change.

> " Go confidently in the direction of your dreams! Live the life you've imagined. As you simplify your life, the laws of the universe will be simpler. "
>
> **—HENRY DAVID THOREAU**

I've heard from many kids over the years who've admitted they owed one or more of their teachers sincere gratitude, apologies, or tributes for the teachers' enormous influence. Do they call? Write? Only rarely. But they think about this person with boundless affection on a monthly, weekly, or even daily basis.

Just because you don't hear from your students doesn't mean your efforts were in vain. Just the opposite. Believe me about this. You've done your best. You *will* be remembered—and cherished.

# 10

## What's Next

"*He called after me, Hey, Mr. McCourt, thanks. I like your class. It's weird, that class, but I figured I might even become a teacher like you.*"

**—Frank McCourt**

Everyone wants to hear about what makes an inspiring teacher.

Someone who is competent, caring, and concerned. Hopeful, enthusiastic, and optimistic. Knowledgeable and approachable. Smart and funny—with an instinct for reaching young people and a talent for making them want to know more, learn faster, and become better.

And then . . . he or she often possesses one or two odd idiosyncrasies that fly directly in the face of all logic. Perhaps a friendly gruffness or an affection for colorful snakes or an over-the-top repertoire of corny jokes. Or maybe he or she prefers large classes.

It isn't supposed to work. But somehow, for that person, it does. What does this teach our kids? That their own particular brands of lunacy can be equally captivating—and successful.

Can every child be reached, then? I believe that he can. But maybe not by you. Maybe by someone else whose unusual approach just happens to snag his attention and suddenly makes him drop all his defenses.

I'm very aware that this book is filled with contradictions. I know I suggest going after your dropouts—but also that for many kids, especially those in vocational programs, twelve years of public schooling may actually be too long. I condemn eighth chances—but I offer plenty of second ones, and then suggest that there's always an opportunity for a student to turn things around. Does that make me illogical or difficult to pin down? I don't think so.

In education there are few absolutes. Every learning experience is filtered through a personal lens. One student may declare your class the biggest waste of time she's ever known. Another may credit you as the sole reason she decided to stay long enough to graduate. Yes, many gifted teachers hear both responses!

All I know for sure, after thirty-one years in the classroom, is that public education, despite its many shortcomings and inequities, is still the closest thing our nation has to a level playing field. No matter where you live, it's the best deal in town. Regardless of whether the facilities are new and snazzy or downright falling apart, education is still the fastest ticket out of a bad home life, a bad upbringing, a bad neighborhood, or a bad attitude. School is where we all can learn to think, to analyze, to debate, to reach logical conclusions, to get along with people who are different. And to plan together for a better future.

The key to all of this? Teachers, of course. An inspiring teacher somehow makes the unworkable workable. And the workable—brilliant. He or she can even convince a student that a destiny far beyond whatever his family or his peers may have charted for him is possible. Who can put a price tag on that?

Yet our government and our citizenry still don't understand. Funding for schools is still woefully inadequate. Teachers are still paying for their own materials. Even those who push carts from class to class or shiver in tin trailers where the wind rattles the walls are told at every election where school levies don't pass that they aren't worth even their paltry $35,000 a year—and that they're grasping and greedy if they plead for more.

Every time we place a teacher in a precarious environment, fighting to rise above it drains huge amounts of his or her energy—which inevitably has an impact on students. Take something as simple as air-conditioning. Would any congressman claim to accomplish anything worthwhile in a tiny, cramped space with thirty other people, where the temperature hits ninety-eight degrees by 10:00 A.M.? Well, teachers and kids do it nearly every early fall and late spring day. Should they have to? Should anyone?

I keep trying to imagine a better scenario, and it looks something like this:

Education as a real priority. Properly funded. One highly qualified teacher, therefore, with the same ten students for the first six to eight years. Each child monitored, but also working at his or her own pace, with independent study actively encouraged from day one.

Over that time, each teacher would get to know each student inside and out. In rare cases of personality conflict, transfers could be arranged, but through a screening committee to limit endless hopscotching. Remedial help would be ready as needed.

Following sixth to eighth grade, with a solid foundation in all subjects, students would move on to a high school curriculum of specialty classes in math, science, English, social studies, foreign language, business, home economics, and some sort of vocational training, where they would continue to work at their own pace. Perhaps every would-be geologist should also know how to install a faucet, and every future gourmet chef should also be able to repair a roof! Some people would graduate within two years, some in five. Nobody would get upset about time frames. They would vary, because everyone learns differently.

Each teacher without question would have his or her own climate-controlled classroom, with enough books, enough resource materials, and enough computers. A well-paid aide. And an attached restroom!

Each day would begin with morning exercise (for teachers too), then breakfast, then classes. One early afternoon period would be free for students to snack, socialize, participate in an elective activity, or do some combination of these, and that would be the only time that they could be called to the office, except for family emergencies. All morning instruction time would be considered sacred, inviolable.

By junior year, students would be dismissed at a reasonable hour, such as 1:00 P.M., so that those who had jobs wouldn't be going to bed after midnight. Communities would enforce limits on how many hours a week (twenty-five?) teenagers are allowed to work. Teachers would stay longer each day to hold conferences and complete paperwork, so there'd be far less to lug home on evenings and weekends.

Parental involvement, begun at first-grade level, would be constant and ongoing. No promotions would take place without quarterly conferences that include the child.

Any student misbehavior, even foul language directed at someone else, would mean an instant parent-teacher-administrator meeting before permitting a return to class. After three or four of these go-rounds, parents would become so weary of taking time off work that they'd strongly "encourage" their offspring to behave properly. The eventual alternative, suspension from school, would become the ultimate dreaded punishment—because it would mean that a student lost valuable class time and took longer to graduate, and a parent would have to wonder what his or her child was doing all day.

Can any teacher or administrator shoot holes in this plan? Certainly. But with gradual modifications, something resembling it might work, and we'd eventually construct a system far more efficient and less resource draining than the one we have now.

The prospect is at least tantalizing enough that it still sometimes keeps me awake at night.

> "Truth is a hard apple, whether one is throwing it or one is catching it."
> **—DONALD BARTHELME**

Meanwhile . . . back in your own classroom, you can do the next best thing: create a private oasis, where every single student feels safe, cherished, and valued. Where your authority is shrink-wrapped by compassion and concern. Where your adult confidence and expertise aren't threatening or demeaning, only another way of showing your kids that one day they too will blossom as professionals who are willing, even eager to contribute their best efforts.

I hope that possibility keeps *you* awake at night.

# About the Author

**Coleen Armstrong** taught secondary English, German, and Spanish in the Hamilton City School District, in Ohio, for thirty-one years. Coleen won both state and national recognition, including Ashland Oil's Teacher Achievement Award and WKRC-TV's Outstanding Teacher Award, and she was named one of five finalists for the National Teachers Hall of Fame.

As a local TV talk-show host, Coleen interviewed prominent personalities and wrote and narrated city-oriented documentaries. She has also published hundreds of articles in newspapers and magazines and is currently a senior contributing home and garden writer for *Cincinnati Magazine*. Coleen's first book, *Please Don't Call My Mother: How Schools and Parents Can Work Together to Get Kids Back on Track* (coauthored with Warren County superintendent John Lazares), was published by Parenting Press in 2001.